WALKING
LONDON
WALL

1 Photograph of London Wall, Trinity Place, 1882

WALKING LONDON WALL

ED HARRIS

The
History
Press

First published 2009

The History Press
The Mill, Brimscombe Port
Stroud, Gloucestershire, GL5 2QG
www.thehistorypress.co.uk

British Library Cataloguing in Publication Data.
A catalogue record for this book is available from the British Library.

ISBN 978 07524 4846 6

Typesetting and origination by The History Press
Printed in Great Britain

Contents

Introduction and Acknowledgements

This is a book of two unequal parts. It is designed for both the armchair rambler and the field explorer. That is, the bulk of the book aims to offer a virtual walk through the history of London's ancient City Wall and the rest is a Field Guide to the physical act. I don't therefore expect the would-be explorer to lug this tome around the perimeter of the Square Mile, pausing perhaps for some considerable time at each location to consult it. That is possible to do, of course. There is many a delightful pub, park, café, restaurant and open space where this might be done, but for those wanting to avail themselves of arguably the best value free day out in the capital, then the guide/aide-mémoire is to be recommended.

It was the myriad disappointments experienced by an American friend of mine visiting London for the first time that gave me the idea to write this first truly definitive guide to its ancient City Wall. A Californian, she was beside herself to find so little remaining of what she imagined London to be. Blue plaques (where there are blue plaques) replace castles and no one wears a bowler hat. My unavailability to act as her guide for the first few days of her visit meant that she had to rely on various guide books. Interested in Roman London, I lent her my copy of the Museum of London's *London Wall Walk*, a guide published in 1984. The City of London, however, as anyone who knows it can testify, is an ever-evolving organism, constantly reinventing itself. So much so that any guidebook loses some of its credibility in a matter of months, let alone twenty-four years. 'You must show me around,' she demanded, having failed miserably to follow the route. 'I want to see the London Wall.'

Most of us who believe we know London think of its ancient Wall as distinct, disparate fragments dotted about the Museum of London and on Tower Hill. Otherwise, there's not a lot to see. Or so we think. In 1974 the author, journalist and broadcaster, Hunter Davies, spent a year tracing Hadrian's Wall across the neck of England, from Wallsend near Newcastle to the Solway. The result was the original and highly successful book *A Walk Along the Wall*. While there are now dozens of books written about Hadrian's Wall, I was amazed to discover not a single one about the second largest construction project in Roman Britain. London's Wall features only lightly in the bigger histories of the capital and to all intents and purposes is deemed unworthy of historical investigation in its own right. So it was that I decided to see for myself what remained of it, and took my American friend to Tower Hill to watch her navigate the route armed only with the Museum of London's guide. Unbeknown to me she had printed off a set of instructions found on the Internet. I said nothing. Finding Bevis Marks for Aldgate via Jewry Street proved taxing. Building works at Bishopsgate didn't stop us reaching London Wall but we did miss out All Hallows-on-the-Wall. Past Moorgate for St Alphage Garden was straightforward, unlike finding a way into the Barbican Centre, for which there is no instruction. After Noble Street where the Museum guide ends, the Internet instructions advised making for St Paul's and turning right before Newgate Street, but not where. At Old Bailey the instructions were to turn left to follow the road to Ludgate where the trail ended, missing out on Blackfriars altogether. Not only was the experience enough to challenge the knowledge of a seasoned London cabbie, but we missed out on much of what remains to see within, without and beneath the labyrinthine passages and alleyways that make up the history of the most fascinating Square Mile on earth.

When it was published, the Museum of London guide complemented twenty-one tiled panels along the route. Some survive as year on year the various faces of the City alter dramatically. Only the ancient street pattern remains largely intact, or is even improved, with each new redevelopment. Negotiating the line of London Wall along an easily defined landmarked route from one decade to another is a perilous task. It is frankly counterproductive for any guide to cite a particular building, as it is likely to be gone or to have been redeveloped on publication. Apart from the River Thames, the only constants on this ever changing landscape are the main players such as the Bank of England, St Paul's Cathedral and the Tower of London. Then there are the railway stations above and under ground. Otherwise, every few months, great chunks of the City streetscape seem to morph into new landmarks that will undoubtedly be replaced within a few short decades.

The City of London is best understood as essentially an arc, a half circle inscribed north of the River Thames with Cannon Street Station on the compass point. This describes the area much as it was founded by the Romans almost 2000 years ago. Inscribing such an arc from left to right, that is in a clockwise direction, throws up an interesting observation. From the earliest times the few chroniclers, antiquaries, scholars, historians and copyists of London history who have recorded the route of London Wall, have all done so in an anti-clockwise direction, that is from Tower Hill, usually ending at Ludgate. It is a format still followed, the seeds planted by John Stow, the Elizabethan historical journeyman in his *Survey of London* written in 1598. John Strype's *Survey of the Cities of London and Westminster* published in 1720 greatly expands on Stow, laying down the core of knowledge for future investigators to call upon. *London Wall Through Eighteen Centuries* is a slim volume issued by the Council for Tower Hill Improvement in 1937. Jointly authored by the historical author, Walter G. Bell, the Investigator to the Society of Antiquaries of London, Frank Cottrill and writer, Charles Spon, its mission was to provide 'a history of the ancient Town Wall' and a survey of the existing remains. The Foreword, written by W.S. Barclay, General Secretary of the Council for Tower Hill Improvement, echoes precisely my own sentiments in wanting to record London's Wall as a specific and important historical feature.

Questions were put to the government in 1936 as to whether it would consider having an authoritative survey made of the remaining portions of the Wall to save it from further destruction, and also to classify what remained as an Ancient Monument. The last time Parliament concerned itself with the ancient fortification was in 1760 when the City Gates were removed. In reply, the Office of Works confirmed that a survey had recently been made of the remains of the Wall at Tower Hill, and that the results of an authoritative survey were recorded in the volume on Roman London published by the Royal Commission on Historical Monuments in England. Suitable portions of London Wall were being considered for scheduling under the Ancient Monuments Acts, the reply continued, including that part of the Wall on Tower Hill.

It is not clear if W.S. Barclay was impressed by this response. He informs the reader that the volume on Roman London was out of print and that unlike other historic features of London, anyone curious to find out about its City Wall would have to visit certain libraries and search many obscure records before assembling even a very basic idea of the subject. 'For, curiously enough,' he adds, 'no book has been published dealing widely with London Wall. Yet in all England there was no civic monument on so large a scale and with such far reaching effects on the life of its citizens'. As recent as 1867, he notes, so little of the London Wall was 'known or heeded', it had been 'pierced at many points for mains, torn up in places for basements' with the old wall yielding its secrets 'slowly and sullenly'. The further question arose, why concern ourselves with something we can't see? 'A Wall that is pulled down or buried is no longer a Wall, except to antiquaries and such-like'. For in 1937, as it was in 1867, as it remains to this day, many a Londoner and visitor is 'unaware even of such portions as the centuries have spared us'.

W.S. Barclay hoped that the surviving fragments of London Wall would be better cared for in future. That was the purpose of the Tower Hill Improvement Council and others interested in London antiquities. The Council was set up by the Reverend Philip T.B. Clayton, founder of the Christian welfare organisation Toc H, in 1932, after he was appointed Vicar of All Hallows on Tower Hill ten years earlier. 'Tubby', as Dr Clayton was affectionately known, immediately set about improving the lot of this historical quarter then heavily industrialised with few facilities for local people, visitors and tourists. He gained among others an invaluable ally in Lord Wakefield of Hythe, a former Lord Mayor of London and Proprietor of Castrol Oil who was committed to public service and to upholding the prestige of the City. The movement rapidly grew into a large and active organisation with Royal patronage and achieved much in the way of improvement and perception of the district. The Wakefield Gardens we enjoy today were created when active steps were taken to preserve and display the section of City Wall at Tower Hill.

London Wall Through Eighteen Centuries was written as much as a celebration of the Wall as to raise the profile of the project. By the 'happy collaboration' of the eminent antiquaries of the day, the story of London's Wall was 'presented for the first time as a separate entity', except that it was limited to as much of the Wall where it could be found and in no easy order for the lay-explorer to follow. Its value increases, however, within the context of *The Old Wall of the City of London*, an illustrated paper written by Norman Cook, Keeper of the Guildhall Museum in 1951, six years after great chunks of London Wall were unearthed by enemy bombs. Cook likewise begins at the Tower of London and ends at Noble Street. Between these two areas the visitor could either walk, or having inspected the remains of the Wall extending from the Tower, take a bus across the City to Cripplegate.

Investigating the route of the Wall from west to east, that is in a clockwise direction, proves not only more instinctive, but serves to provide a gentler and more accessible introduction to the City of London in the historical, topographical and geographical sense. As well as taking full advantage of its many meanders and secret passages, it's a more dramatic affair. By that I mean where there is little to see of London Wall in the physical sense until after Ludgate, so much of London's history is covered in this rich corner, what lies underfoot is just as potent as the physical remains to be marvelled at later. Like any good production the route shifts seamlessly from the Prologue and the opening Acts to the main body of the work, saving the best until last as we return to the Thames and the most illustrious fortification in the world, the Tower of London. Of the many supporting roles, some remain half-hidden and others are added to the cast list with each new discovery. Decade by decade, each time a City street is dug up or another building demolished, so a different facet of the capital emerges or a fresh perspective is found. The only constant is London's Wall. As such the provision of a single coherent account of it is, to my mind at least, long overdue.

First I would like to extend my grateful thanks to the Museum of London Archaeological Service, the London and Middlesex Archaeological Service and to the Society of Antiquaries, whose reports and observations over many years have provided the hooks upon which to hang my humble observations. In particular I would like to thank the following who have patiently and courteously answered my further enquiries and provided information: Mr S.F. Jones, Central Criminal Court; Jackie Kielty, Department of Early London History and Collections Museum of London; Andrew Todd and Karen Condon, Merrill Lynch; Jane Miller, Sir John Cass Foundation; Peter Prescott, The Wine Library; Bill McCann, Fleet Valley Project, Museum of London; Keith O'Connor, London Metropolitan University; Sharon McLaughlin, Barbican Estate Office; Daniel Imade, Arup Photo Library; Greg Williams, City of London Press Office; Maite Lubian-Grana and William Beaver, Office of the Rt. Hon. The Lord Mayor of London; Bridget Clifford, Keeper of Collections (South), Royal Armouries Museum; Roland Smith. Clerk to the Trustees, Wakefield & Tetley Trust; Helen Kent, Librarian, Information Desk & Library, London Transport Museum; Jane Anderson and Luke Batney, Field Fisher Waterhouse; Chris Saunders, Operations; Comptroller & City Solicitor's Department, City of London Corporation; Melissa Humphrys, London Underground Customer Service Centre; Tracey O'Brien, Senior Press Officer, London Underground Desk, Transport for London; John Reilly, EDF Security; Nick Molnar and Martyn Fawdry, Sir Robert McAlpine Ltd; David Divers of the Greater London Archaeology Advisory Service, English Heritage; Jane Siddell, Inspector of Ancient Monument, English Heritage; to Diane Griffen at virtualpasupport.com, and last but not least to my long-suffering wife, Sue, for maintaining consciousness throughout.

Ed Harris. Whitton, Middlesex. 2008

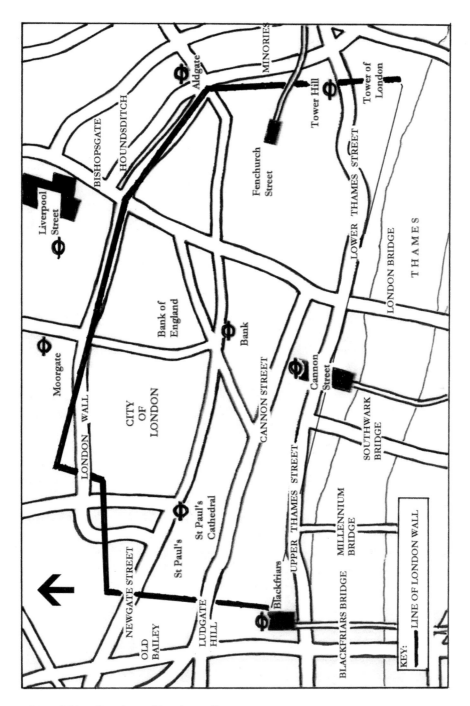

2 Map of City of London and London Wall

PART ONE

London and its Wall
A Brief Overview

Topographical considerations dictated the evolution of London. The Romans built a Thames crossing between the low sandy islands of Southwark and the higher, firmer ground on the north bank where a road led north. Eventually a T-junction came about with the main east–west road fronting a Basilica and Forum according to the common pattern of Roman town planning. This main east–west road was established as early as AD 47 and led to Calleva (Silchester) and Verulamiurn (St Albans), crossing the Walbrook river, which divided the Roman settlement in two. The Fleet tributary bounded the town on its west side. A secondary road system was built before the time of the Boudican revolt of AD 60/1 about where Cheapside runs today. This revolt by the indigenous population resulted in a serious setback to the development of London, but also led to its flourishing as the provincial capital. Development took place on the previously sparsely populated higher ground in the northwest (around Guildhall and the Barbican). Here, full-scale reclamation and drainage of the upper Walbrook valley began between AD 90 and AD 200 when the fort at Cripplegate was incorporated into a defensive wall that would physically limit the growth of London for almost 1500 years.

The line of the Wall that once encircled the City of London measured about 9 miles. Opinion differs as to when the first wall was built, but there is no doubt of its Roman origin. Henry of Huntington, the English historian who became Archdeacon of Huntingdon in about 1110, credits the Empress Helen, wife of the Roman general Constantius Chlorus, Emperor of Britain, Gaul and Spain. But this isn't documented elsewhere or evident in the many finds to date strongly indicating that the Wall was begun in the second century AD. Charles Roach Smith, the eminent nineteenth-century antiquary and Secretary of the Archaeological Society of London, believed that the first wall enclosed a much smaller Londinium just east of Monument underground station with the north wall running along Cornhill and Leadenhall Street and the eastern flank towards Lower Thames Street. The western boundary, he suggests, was east of Walbrook, close to Cannon Street

Station. There is some evidence to back this up. When the Emperor Hadrian visited Londinium in AD 122, the City had yet to extend to its full size to the west where second-century burials have been found inside the later line of the City Wall.

There is another theory based on the dating evidence of Roman bricks that the Wall was built earlier than is now widely acknowledged, possibly several decades earlier. But then bricks and other building materials have been reused throughout history and the Romans especially made good use of them to construct stronger and hardier walls. Old bricks and building rubble were used to build Rome's City Wall, begun in AD 271. Unlike London's Wall, that protecting the heart of the empire was entirely faced with brick, as were its towers and most of its gateways. These bricks were commonly crude or unbaked blocks. Walling tiles were developed from pottery; thin in substance they were made of heavy clay, tempered and long exposed. These were used not only as bonding courses, but for the entire substance of walls, which leads to some confusion when talking of Roman tiles or bricks. They were interchangeable, with a tile, including roofing tiles, used both for their intended purpose as well as used in walling. The tile courses in London Wall were bonds, but they also divided it into strata locking up the moisture of the mortar from too-rapid absorption and evaporation. The construction of Rome's wall and associated clearance involved the ruthless demolition of a large number of buildings, including suburban villas, tombs and even imperial palaces, all of which supplied building materials. William Richard Lethaby, the celebrated nineteenth- and twentieth-century architectural historian, paints a graphic picture of the traveller approaching the turreted walls of Londinium through 'the gardens of the dead' as far as the City Ditch. Just as Rome was straddled by a great belt of cemeteries, so was each side of the main roads leading from the City Gates of Londinium, extending from Spitalfields in the east across Moorfields to the Fleet valley by Ludgate. These cities of the dead must have been impressive, as well as beautiful, filled with columns, sculptures, mausolea and altar tombs, profusely carved and even coloured. Perhaps similar recycling took place when building London's Wall; otherwise there is very little archaeological evidence to date it precisely. Fragments of monuments from the east side of the City are found in the area of Tower Hill, those from north of the City in Camomile Street, Houndsditch and other bastions and relics found at Ludgate and Newgate originated west of the City.

It was in the year 55 BC that Julius Caesar first crossed the Channel with a force of around 10,000 soldiers, but had to retreat due to bad weather holding up a reserve force from France. The following year Caesar landed again at Deal in Kent with a force of around 27,000 infantry and cavalry. They marched inland to be met by a large force of Britons north of the River Thames, which they eventually defeated. In September the Romans left Britain to deal with problems in Gaul, leaving a presence in Britain in the form of trade links. In May AD 43 a Roman force of about 40,000 once again landed in Kent. They defeated a force of Britons and began taking the south-east of Britain. By the autumn, the Roman Emperor Claudius arrived with reinforcements. The fortress of Camulos was taken, making way for the eventual establishment of the provincial capital of Camulodunum (Colchester).

By AD 47 the Romans had conquered the whole of southern Britain and claimed it as part of the Empire. Between AD 47 and AD 50 a great trading post was established 60 miles to the south of the capital on the north bank of a wide, meandering river cutting deep from the sea into the south-east of the country. That river was the Thames and this place would become known as Londinium.

With no archaeological evidence to support any view or theory expressed, we simply do not know if this was the site of an existing settlement or established Iron Age ford crossing the River Thames. It does, however, seem highly unlikely that such an attractive site had never previously been settled. Forty miles from the sea, its location at the tidal limit of the river (as it was at that time) would have made it ideal for seagoing vessels to sail upstream against the strong current. Coming upriver it represented one of the first sites on the north bank where there was a large area of firm, dry ground. It was also flanked both sides by tributaries of the Thames and was protected to the north by a vast expanse of boggy marsh; all in all, the ideal riverside settlement. We can be reasonably sure that by AD 60 the population of Roman Londinium numbered in the tens of thousands. Here was set up the office of the procurator Decianus, the emperor's agent. Many merchants too, from all the far-flung areas of the empire set up in Londinium for business. With secure frontiers established and south-east England holding the promise of long-term peace, this security and stability made it an attractive proposition for continental merchants and Roman bankers to invest heavily in trade with Britain and to develop the new great centre of commerce. That is until other indigenous tribes joined Queen Boudica and her Iceni to rid the land of the invaders. London at this time had no walls. The archaeological evidence of the catastrophe that enveloped the city in AD 60 makes what happened dramatically clear, the foundations of the City when excavated identified by a layer of red and black burned ash and soot. Once the rebellious Britons were defeated, it was decided that the hitherto undistinguished Londinium made for a better capital than Colchester on military and commercial grounds. The new capital quickly expanded into a rich and powerful metropolis with splendid temples, mansions, a forum and basilica, a palace, an amphitheatre and baths. By AD 125 a fort was built to the north-west, which was incorporated into the City Wall when it was built seventy-five years later.

Enough of the Roman City Wall has been preserved or recorded to be sure about the method of its construction and the materials used: as much as 90,000 tons of Kentish ragstone quarried somewhere in the Maidstone district, perhaps from Boughton Monchelsea or Allington, where Roman remains have been found quite close to ancient stone quarries. The base of the external face at ground level boasted a chamfered plinth made of a brown, ferruginous sandstone, probably also of Kentish origin. The skilled work was probably done at the quarries in shaping over a million squared facing stones and 5,000 chamfered plinths. As many again limestone coping stones with curved upper surfaces, probably from the Cotswolds, were required for gate, turret and parapet battlements. Huge crane systems must have been in place probably along the riverside as work progressed, with dockers offloading the cargo onto fleets of wagons. But the south-east of Britain was suffering a drop in the population at this time, so workers may have been drafted in. Very few towns in the north-western provinces had city walls, making the decision to do so at such a time all the more intriguing. Once the materials were on site, the Wall was laid on either a foundation of flints and paddled clay, packed into a trench dug in the natural soil 3–4ft deep, or in soft waterlogged ground where special measures were taken to ensure stability by using oak piles. Onto the flint and clay base was laid the bottom of the mortared superstructure, complete with brick-lined culverts where necessary for drainage. The chamfered plinth about 10in high was laid on the external face of the base. On the back, or the internal face on a level with the plinth, was laid a course of three bricks, with a step or offset of about 3in between the top and middle brick. The thickness of the Wall at this level varies from 7–9ft. The bricks are not brick as we know them, but more of a tile, usually red, hard-fired and of the common Roman shape, being one and a half inches thick, eleven and a half inches wide, and the same long. On both faces of the Wall the blocks of ragstone are squared and laid in regular courses, while the core consists of ragstone rubble. Bonding courses of brick are laid through the thickness of the Wall, so that they appear on both faces. These courses, a well-known feature of Roman building, have a reinforcing effect. In the London Wall they are triple, that is to say their thickness is composed of three layers of bricks laid flat, one above another, or more commonly, double. Above the plinth are four courses of facing stones about 2ft high, then a triple bonding course and then six more courses of stone for a height of 3ft. A double bonding course, five more courses, another double bonding course, and so on. At each bonding course there is an offset of about 3in on the internal face, so that the structure is reduced in thickness as it ascends.

The Wall may have been built in sections by gangs, perhaps working independently to some extent, as the thickness and spacing of the bonding courses vary from place to place. The existence of gates may have a bearing on this, but generally the Wall as a whole, apart from later Roman and medieval additions, is clearly a work of one design and one period. And then there is the aesthetic aspect to consider. As Walter G. Bell noted in 1937: 'When we see the regularly laid courses – in which the grey of the ragstone contrasts with the red of the bricks and the warm brown of the plinth – we realise that the builders had an eye for decorative effect, and their work, appearing now as it often does amid drab surroundings, looks up with the alien air of a more colourful age'. The Wall defences were later further strengthened with the addition of over twenty semi-circular shaped bastions, or fortified towers.

Twenty-one bastions are identified on a map of London Wall drawn up by James Spon for the Tower Hill Improvement Council in 1936, starting at the Wardrobe Tower in the Tower of London and ending just north of Ludgate, to which another six assumed sites have been subsequently added. The building of these bastions must have generated the modification of other existing structures in the City Wall, possibly the internal turrets and the gates with similar projections serving the same purpose, to provide an effective system of crossfire. Aldgate certainly had these bastion-like projections, although probably not until the Middle Ages. Normally the addition

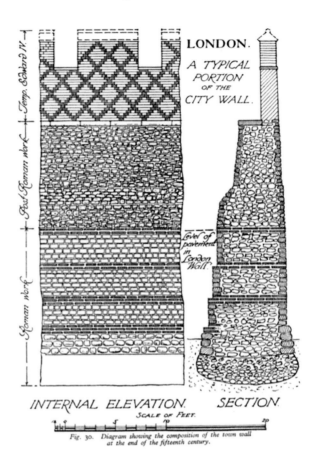

LONDON.

A TYPICAL PORTION OF THE CITY WALL.

INTERNAL ELEVATION.   *SECTION.*

SCALE OF FEET.

Fig. 30.   Diagram showing the composition of the town wall at the end of the fifteenth century.

3 Diagram showing composition of London Wall (from *Roman London*)

of bastions required the digging of a new and wider ditch, usually flat-bottomed, somewhat further away from the wall. This was not only a replacement for the old City Ditch but an integral part of the late Roman defensive system, keeping the attackers under fire for longer from the bastions. This was in turn mostly destroyed by the even wider City Ditch dug in the thirteenth century.

The remains of a few bastions, later built onto the Wall, survive along the route of London Wall. Up to twenty of them have been recorded, placed at regular intervals. The method of construction, built against the external face of the Wall and not linked to it, is evidence that these additions formed no part of the original defensive scheme. Whereas the Wall belongs to the early second century, some of the bastions are attributed to the late Roman period, the third or fourth century when there was reason for a strengthening of the City's defences in accordance with the latest tactical ideas. Others were added in the medieval period. In the late third century when the Saxons began their raids on the southern and eastern shores, forts were built as part of a scheme of defence designed to meet the new danger. Many of these, such as Richborough in Kent, Pevensy in Sussex and Porchester in Hampshire, have bastions similar to those defending London.

Thus the building of them falls into two camps, marking distinct differences in construction. Those to the east of the City are generally considered to be of an earlier date than those to the west. The Riverside Wall may have been constructed at the same time as the eastern group of bastions extending from Tower Hill to the crossing of the Walbrook by All Hallows church. These were solidly built, incorporating re-stones from older buildings and monuments, decorated architectural fragments and tombstones. Between All Hallows and Cripplegate no remains of bastions have been found, probably because the marshy ground to the north of the City at this point was considered defensively sufficient. The bastions of the group after Cripplegate contained no reused material and the work of the medieval builder is easily distinguished from that of the Roman. Two of the best examples survive in the old churchyard of St Giles' Cripplegate and of the three exposed between Newgate and Aldersgate, the remains of one, complete with a piece of Wall, survives under the Merrill Lynch Financial Centre in Giltspur Street. On the east side of the Wall as far as Moorgate, with the exception of the Wardrobe Tower in the Tower of London, all of the bastions are solid at the base and contain re-used stones, fragments of ruined buildings and monuments. The other bastions west from Moorgate, with one exception, are hollow on the base and, like the wall itself, contain no reused materials. None are as old as the Wall, nor are part of the original design, but were all later built up against the completed Wall, as evidenced by the plinth running through them without interruption and other factors.

Until the late 1970s the Roman Riverside Wall was considered by many to be a 'fiction'. Even now there is room for doubt in some peoples' minds. We cannot be certain of its exact build date, but some features of its construction, such as the incorporation of reused stones, may be paralleled in the building of the eastern bastions, and it is not unreasonable to suggest that both were built at the same time, probably no earlier than the third century AD. The use of a pink-coloured mortar is another clue. The Romans made formidably fine mortar and concrete, careful to use clean coarse gravel and finely divided lime. They also used crushed tile and pottery for special work, making the mortar appear quite red. At Richborough Castle in Kent the facing stones throughout are cemented with a much finer mortar than that used on the interior, where powdered tile is used. The advantage of this is that the mortar absorbs and holds water, allowing it to dry very slowly to harden more effectively. This is as evident in the construction of bastions stepped into the town ditch as it is all along the Riverside Wall. Both fortifications were probably constructed a layer at a time over long lengths, so as to have been available as a defence at an early stage and without the need for scaffolding. For the foundations a channel some 100ft wide had to be cleared, cut and filled with flint and puddled clay, and, where the ground was especially soft, supported on a rock raft with wooden piles. Some of the spoil would be used to create an earth bank against the interior face of the Wall. The logistics would have been much the same. An immense quantity of ragstone and the larger sandstone blocks had to be quarried, shaped and carted to the River Medway

4 Diagram of example
bastion at Le Mans and
Senlis

where they were loaded onto ships and barges for the relatively short journey
to Londinium via the Thames estuary. As well as lime for burning to make the
mortar, clay was dug for brick-making and wood cut for firing and construction
in the small industrial sites outside the City limits. Throughout the third and
fourth centuries, however, the seaborne attacks by Saxon pirates sailing up the
Thames became bolder and more frequent. The Empire itself, staggered with the
shock of barbarian invasions along all its frontiers and eventually the Roman
garrison, was forced to leave Britain in order to defend Rome. Many a rich citizen
fled the otherwise heavily fortified provincial capital as the Saxons spread ever
closer. The decline in London-minted coins shows the falling-off in trade after the
first quarter of the fourth century as the last of the legions sailed away.

By AD 600 the new invaders had settled as farmers, with most of south-east
England a Saxon country. A Saxon king ruled Kent from Canterbury, and another
Essex from London. In AD 604, the first Christian cathedral dedicated to St Paul
was built on the low plateau sloping south to the Thames foreshore and west to the
banks of the River Fleet. The wooden structure burned down in AD 675 and was
rebuilt ten years later, only to be destroyed by Vikings in AD 962. A new cathedral
church was then built in stone. Between AD 600 and 800 a London trading pattern
that persists to this day was initiated by the Jutes, a Germanic tribe who invaded
Britain in the fifth century AD. There were goldsmiths from Ghent, clothiers from
Flanders and Cologne and wine traders from Lorraine. But then, from about
AD 800, the same river that had brought about the largest trading settlement in
England provided passage for a fresh and even more ferocious invader than the

Saxons – the Vikings. In AD 839 a fleet of Danish ships sailed up the Thames, plundered and burned London, and withdrew unharmed. On the high seas, too, Viking ships repeatedly attacked and plundered the Saxon vessels plying between London and the Continent. London went into eclipse once more. Enter King Alfred.

King Alfred the Great is considered the first king of England. He became ruler of the West Saxons after he and his brother defeated the Danes in the Battle of Ashdown in Berkshire. He became king following the death of his brother Ethelred in AD 871. In AD 886 Alfred freed London from Danish occupation and a treaty was made with King Guthrum and the East Anglians, dividing England. The walls of London were repaired, the town was repopulated with new settlers, and a street plan inaugurated that survives in part to this day. Otherwise the archaeological evidence for Alfred's London is slight. His most decisive victory came in AD 895 when he led an army against the fleet of Danish ships being towed up the River Lea towards London. But again and again during the tenth century the Vikings attacked London. In AD 994 Olaf Tryggvason, later King of Norway, tried to break down part of London Bridge, but was beaten off. In 1010 the Saxon King, Ethelred II, successfully defended London.

Despite all these violent upheavals, foreign merchants continued to come upriver to do business in London and to settle near the shore. Wine merchants from Rouen built their own dock for their cargoes and were followed by merchants of Genoa and Flanders. The Vikings too eventually stayed to trade and in 1016 their warrior king, Canute, a Christian, became King of England in addition to most of Scandinavia. Fifty years later, when the Normans arrived in Britain, William the Conqueror was careful not to offend the leading citizens of London but to win them over. Once established, he started to develop the strategic defensive position on the Thames first set up by the Romans. Here he would build the imposing White Tower, the nucleus of the Tower of London, an outward symbol of royal power always to be resented in the City. William's castle has never at any time been regarded as part of the City; rather an outpost of royal authority designed to keep the citizens in check as well as to protect them. In the words of the Elizabethan historian, John Stow, the Tower was 'a citadel to command or defend the City, a royal palace, a prison of state, the only place of coinage for England, an armoury, a treasury'.

In 1826 the manuscript of an untitled poem about William of Normandy's conquest of England was discovered by German historian, Georg Heinrich Pertz, who identified it as the *Carmen de Hastingae Proelio* (*proello*), or *Song of the Battle of Hastings*. It is variously attributed to Guy, Bishop of Amiens before 1086, or deemed a twelfth-century historical 'literary exercise' of no historical value. Some academics argue that it can be 'securely identified' as the work of Bishop Guy, probably from 1067. Others suggest that it was borrowed by William of Poitiers for his account of the life of William the Conqueror, or the *Carmen* borrowed from it, or again that the two are the result of a common source.

William of Poitiers describes an outbreak of severe dysentery amongst the Norman forces at Dover. Leaving the sick behind, Duke William moved on to Canterbury, which submitted to him. The following day, although falling ill himself at a place called the 'Broken Tower', the advance continued towards London where English forces emerged but were 'driven back within the walls' by William's advance guard of 500 knights. The *Carmen* describes London as being protected on the left side (the north) by walls and on the right (the south) side by the river and 'neither fears enemies nor dreads being taken by storm'. Such a description suggests an approach on the City from the west, the Riverside Wall thought to have almost entirely collapsed by this time. Of the capture of London, the *Carmen* tells us that the Duke's men encamped around the City Walls while he took up residence in King Edward's Hall at Westminster. Siege engines were constructed and when diplomatic efforts failed, Edgar the Ætheling (the boy) surrendered the City to William who was duly crowned at Westminster Abbey on Christmas Day 1066.

As well as all the outward symbols of Norman superiority and dominance there was a great accounting process, an inventory that sought to catalogue all that this conquered land contained. Most modern historians believe that it was in the late summer of 1086, that a scribe working for the Bishop of Durham began writing the bulk of what was then called the *Book of Winchester*. With a dedication to detail worthy of any twenty-first century political machine, he gifted succeeding generations with an astonishing window into life in early medieval England. This enormous work set out to record who did and owned what, and who worked for whom in all the villages and manors throughout the land, and most importantly, what taxes and dues they paid. Ultimately set out in over 800 pages it contained 13,418 place names, almost 90 per cent of which are still in existence. The later *Anglo-Saxon Chronicle* claims that 'not even one ox, nor one cow, nor one pig' escaped notice, although this was not strictly the case. The plan was to assemble a contemporary account of what each manor was called, who held it at the time of King Edward and after the conquest, its size, value and how many tenants, villagers and others who worked the woodlands, meadows, pastures, mills and fisheries. The completed version became known as the Domesday Book. This most famous piece of written British documentation is not, however, comprehensive. As well as (understandable) errors in geography, it excludes counties north of the River Tees, then mostly in control of the Scots, and crucially to this account, much of London and the county of Middlesex in which it sits. Even Winchester, then the capital, is omitted. So, we may never know what Norman London looked like and who controlled what. It wasn't until 1191 when Prince John granted recognition of the City as a corporate body that its recorded history really begins.

Among local authorities the Corporation of London is unique. Not only is it the oldest in the country, combining its ancient traditions and ceremonial functions with the role of a modern and efficient authority, but it operates on a non-party political basis through its Lord Mayor. Before joining the crusade, King Richard appointed as Chancellor William Longchamps, a Norman of humble origin who, though loyal to Richard, scorned everything English. His burdensome taxation aroused such a storm of discontent that the English Barons and the burgesses of the City decided to remove him and to appoint Prince John as Regent. Later, as King, John was himself forced to sign a peace treaty with the Barons who were in revolt against his disastrous foreign policy and arbitrary government. John was forced to concede certain rights at Runnymede in 1215, when the Magna Carta restored to the City of London its ancient liberties and free customs. A new Mayor was to be elected annually who would present himself to the sovereign for approval every year after his election. Since this was not always convenient, John's successor, Henry III, gave permission for the Mayor to present himself to his Barons of the Exchequer at Westminster. At first this was little more than a procession from the City to Westminster, the Mayor being accompanied by guild members and by minstrels playing dignified music. Today we are more familiar with it as the annual Lord Mayor's Show.

In AD 785 Offa, King of Mercia granted a charter to the church of St Peter in Thorney, a reedy island in the Thames 2 miles west of London. Here the first King Harold, a son of Canute the Dane, was buried in 1040. By refounding and improving the original Abbey of St Peter, and building very near it the Palace of Westminster, two centres of power well upriver from the older settlement of London were established. All future kings would be crowned in the Abbey and all future sovereigns until the time of Henry VIII made their homes in the Palace of Westminster. From then until the present day, the history of London as a great metropolis has been dominated by the shifts of power between these two groupings along the river; that of Court and Church at Westminster and the City and Port of London. Just as the City needed the protection of royal power and of charters to conduct its activities successfully, so the Crown in turn needed the wealth, resources, industrial strength and maritime contacts of the City. The most concrete example of this rivalry is the Tower of London, still a royal palace.

It was in 1215, after the Barons had entered London, that they 'with great Diligence, repaired the Walls and the Gates of the City with Stones taken from the Jews broken Houses'. On his succession a year later, Henry III built on this work, causing 'the Walls of London, which were sore decayed, and destitute of Towers to be repaired in more seemly wise than before, at the common Charge of the City'. Edward I, on succession to the throne in 1272, granted Robert Kilwarby, Archbishop of Canterbury, Licence to the Black Friars' church to tear down part of the Roman Wall from Ludgate to the Thames to build a new enclosure from the east bank of the River Fleet to the Thames. To pay for this he granted Henry Wallis, Mayor, and the Citizens of London the right to charge a toll on all goods passing through the Gates of London, reminding them that:

> we have granted you for Aid of the Work of the Walls of our City, and the Closure of the same, divers Customs of vendible Things, coming to the said City, to be taken for a certain Time, We command you, that you cause to be finished the Wall of the said City, now begun near the Friars Preachers, and a certain good and comely Tower at the Head of the said Wall within the Water of the Thames, &c.

As well as the basics such as grain, cheese and butter, these 'vendible things' included lead, wax, almonds, pepper, ginger, frankincense, 'brasil', quicksilver, vermilion, verdigris (dye), cummin, allum, zubar (bronze), liquorice, aniseed, brimstone, copper, resin, calamus (aromatic root), figs, raisins and also 'a great Number of Commodities more, each their Customs,' that defy definition. Moreover, one penny was charged for 'every Hogshead of Beer going out of London to the Parts beyond Sea,' two pennies for 'every Mill to grind Things to be sold' and 'forty shillings one penny for every Horse to be sold and every bull and cow etc.'

Many such proclamations were issued from 1307 and throughout the first twelve years of Edward II's reign, until the flow of provisions into the City slowed down as a direct result of the charges, causing all manner of inconveniences. Also the tax, or 'murage' as it was called, was not entirely applied to the repair of the Walls, but to other works set by the King. Sergeants at the gates collected murage. Those appointed in Edward I's reign were required to be 'skilful men and fluent of speech.' They were also charged to keep a good watch upon persons coming in and going out, 'so that no evil may befall the city.' The Keeper of Newgate was appointed by Edward II to repair the gate's chamber and enclosure, using the proceeds of the tax, but overall little benefit appears to have accrued. For in 1387 King Richard II was proclaiming 'the Walls, and other Forts of the said City' had become 'old and weak' and for want of repair had even collapsed in some places. Nevertheless the watch at the gates, of vital importance to the city's safe keeping, was maintained. A few men sufficed in times of peace, but when invasion threatened, or revolt was feared, the guard was greatly enlarged. In 1381 – the year of Wat Tyler's Rebellion – the order went out to the aldermen of the different wards to provide an armed guard, both day and night, of fifty men for Newgate, and the same numbers for Cripplegate and Bishopsgate. At other gates a smaller guard was called up, but nowhere did the strength fall below twenty-two archers and billmen. Alderman Robert Fabyan, the London Chronicler, was among those called to guard the City Gates in 1497, when a second Cornish uprising looked to halt the extortionate taxes levied to help fight a war against Scotland. Their inspiration was a young man who had appeared in the courts of Europe six year earlier claiming to be Richard, Duke of York, the younger of the two princes believed murdered in the Tower of London. His claim to the English throne, like the perceived threat to London, came to nothing. Fabyan and the other guardians of the City were stood down after the young pretender, later known as Perkin Warbeck, was dragged through the streets from the Tower to Tyburn where he was hanged.

The circuit of the Wall as it appeared in the sixteenth century is described by John Stow in his *Survey of London* (1598), 'to wit, from the Tower of London in the east unto Aldgate, is 83 perches [approx 456yds/417m]. From Aldgate to Bishopsgate, 86 perches, from Bishopsgate in the north to the postern of Cripplegate, 163 perches, from Cripplegate to Aldersgate, 75 perches, from Aldersgate to Newgate, 66 perches and from Newgate in the west to Ludgate, 42 perches, measuring in total: 513 perches' (2821yds/2579m). From Ludgate to the River Fleet was about 330yds/301m and from the Fleet Bridge south to the

River Thames about the same. Every perch consists of 5.5yds, which, according to Stow: 'do yield 3536 yards and a half, containing 10,608 feet, which make up two English miles, and more by 608 feet.' But the influence of the City of London extends beyond this now largely invisible boundary. John Strype, the ecclesiastical historian and biographer, in his hugely expanded version of *Stow's Survey of London* in 1720, describes this other 'Skirt of Ground without the Wall' that enjoys the Liberty or Freedom of the City while separating it from the County of Middlesex. More than 300 acres are contained in a highly irregular arc stretching west from Blackfriars to Temple Law Courts and north to where Fleet Street meets the Strand at the site of Temple Bar Gate. From there the boundary continues north towards Chancery Lane into Holborn and then by means of a hugely circuitous route east via Hatton Garden, Smithfield, Moorgate, Finsbury, Bishopsgate, Spitalfields and Whitechapel to abut the Liberties of the Tower. This area is marked out by the City of London boundary dragons, those fierce silver beasts that sit astride plinths with upswept wings and arrowhead tongues, clutching shields bearing the red cross of St George and short sword of St Paul.

In front of the original Roman Wall, and separated from it by a 'berm', a level space 10–15ft wide, was a defensive ditch about the same width. This was originally cut into V-shape to a depth of about 5ft. In common with other defensive works of its period, the Wall had an earthen ramp piled up on the inside taken from the foundation trench and the ditch. This, and any older Roman ditches that may have existed, were destroyed in medieval times during enhancements to the original City Wall defences. A fragment may have been observed during excavations carried out in 1987 at 41–43 Ludgate Hill where evidence was found of a re-cut V-shaped ditch dated to the tenth or eleventh centuries aligned north–south, the line of the original Roman City Wall. This same excavation also uncovered a 7m length of the later thirteenth-century east–west aligned extension with a foundation arch used to carry the wall over the east bank of the earlier ditch. With no record of the original Roman, Saxon and Norman excavations, all traces have been lost to the medieval work, which was re-cut a number of times until it was eventually filled. Strype tells us that, in the reign of King Richard I (1189–1199), as a result of the threat posed by John, the king's brother, 'earth was taken away to a great Depth and Breadth, and a Ditch made to contain much Water'. The citizens appeared none too keen to complete, finishing the job on 15 October 1213. On numerous occasions over the centuries, the City Ditch became 'exceedingly filled with dirt, dunghills, and other filth', presenting a more real and tangible danger to the City and its inhabitants than war or civil unrest. It was against this 'manifest disgrace and scandal of us and the whole City' that King Richard II extended the right of citizens to charge for all merchandise brought into London for a period of ten years.

In all the ordinances issued by the Parliament of the Interregnum dealing with the fresh fortification of the City and suburbs in 1642 and 1643, the 'Town Ditch' is nowhere mentioned. Yet the Wall as an inner line of defence was still regarded as of value. In 1642, Parliament ordered that 'all sheds and buildings contiguous to London Wall without be taken down, and that the City Wall with its bulwarks, be not only repaired and mounted with artillery but that likewise divers new works be added to the same at places most exposed'. When John Strype published his expanded *Survey of London* sixty years later there were no ditches or bogs in the City except for the Fleet and the remnants of the Walbrook. Instead there were large common drains and sewers built to carry away waste between the 'two Tower-hills' in the east into the Thames and from Ludgate in the west into the Fleet. The ditch being thus filled up, many of the citizens of London with land abutting the City Wall continued the practise of building houses or enclosing yards as much as 16ft on either side of it. So great were these encroachments on land otherwise reserved for the repair and maintenance of the Wall that by this time it was rare to find any part of it untouched. A committee appointed for the letting of the City Lands, ordered a Survey of the entire Wall on both sides to determine the full extent of these encroachments and by whom. A Mr Leybourn undertook the survey, which he delivered to the City Magistrates in the Guildhall. It contained the names of all the occupants and the extent of their holdings. Leaseholders with land abutting the Wall on either side were required to pay a rent commensurate with what the improvements were thought to be worth.

As well as private developments, there were many places on both sides of the Wall designated to be of 'publick Use and Concern'. Between the Tower-Liberty and Aldgate, in a place formerly called 'Vine-Yard' was built a row of houses with stables and haylofts used by the Carmen (goods drivers) working for the City Corporation. The churchyard of St Botolph-without-Bishopsgate had spread over the former ditch as far as the Wall. The church, churchyard and parsonage of St All Hallows had become one with the Wall. Opposite Moorgate was a 'most stately and magnificent Structure' measuring 540ft in length. This was the 'Hospital for Lunaticks', or New Bethlehem, more grimly known as 'Bedlam', which replaced the older asylum on the same site. As well as having the Company of Lorimers livery hall built into it, the Wall was also used to flank the City's grisly store yard used for 'the laying up of Timber, Stone, Gibbets, Pillories, Sledges, and such like Things, for the Execution of Malefactors.' It was also used as an early vehicle pound 'to receive such Carts, Coaches, Horses, &c. as have committed any Offence, or Abuse within the City or Liberties.' The churchyards belonging to the parishes of St Alphage, St Giles Cripplegate, St Olave, Silver-street and St Botolph Aldersgate were all spread to the Wall, with that belonging to Christ's Hospital and the children's recreation yard by Aldersgate for years known as the 'Town Ditch'. The Press Yard belonging to Newgate Prison, the garden and Library belonging to the College of Physicians and that of Justice Hall, more commonly known as the Sessions House, all devoured sections of the Wall.

Daniel Defoe in his *Journal of the Plague Year* (1772) utilises the fictional 'H.F.' (an Aldgate saddler and dissenter) to narrate the historical events of London in 1665 as they unfold. In this, London's ancient wall is observed as having almost mystical powers. People believed for a long time, so H.F. notes that the plague would not come through the City Wall. Having tracked its progress to the exact moment it breaches the City Wall, he, like most Londoners, remained confident that the City Fathers would ensure less suffering to those inside than those outside its protection. Bevis Marks, inside the Wall, managed to escape the horrors of the Great Plague with no deaths recorded. On the other side, across the rank ditch and down the Whitechapel Road, the death rate stood at 80 per cent of the population. Far fewer deaths were recorded within the Square Mile, giving some credence to Daniel Defoe's fictional dissenter. In his *Tour through the Whole Island of Great Britain* (1724–27) Defoe records London spreading 'in a most straggling, confused manner, out of all shape, uncompact, and unequal: neither long or broad, round or square' and looks to the ideal of a regular shape in the form of a fortified wall. Indeed, after the Great Fire, both John Evelyn and Christopher Wren expressed their passion to take the ancient City Wall as the central theme of London's renaissance. Alas, their romantic ideals were not universally embraced, even following the Great Fire that laid bare a huge swathe of the Wall's western section together with most of the City it once served to protect. Defoe's *Colonel Jack* features London's City Wall as a site of contention between traditional civic power and the challenge of the suburbs, but with a significantly changed focus, one more in tune with the king's exhortation to Parliament in 1721, to extend 'our commerce upon which the riches and grandeur of this nation chiefly depend.' Jack, illegitimate and abandoned by his parents, is raised by his foster mother in a poor district outside the Wall east of Aldgate. This serves to determine the relationship with the City and those outside its limits. Jack learns to steal. First in a small way just outside the City precincts at Bartholomew Fair, then inside the Wall where the big money was to be made in almost a parody of the omnipresent economic reality of the City of London.

Much of London's Wall was either demolished in the eighteenth and nineteenth centuries or incorporated into contemporary building schemes. Writing in 1878, Walter Thornbury recalls within living memory huge, shapeless masses of London Wall with trees sprouting from its remains. At the end of the eighteenth century large portions of the Wall were traceable in many places, 'but time has devoured almost the last morsels of that great pièce de résistance', he laments. Perversely, it is mainly as a result of devastating German bombing during the Second World War that the not insubstantial fragments hidden from Thornbury's view are uncovered today. Nothing survives of the gates, however except only Temple Bar, which was returned to the City limits on a site next to St Paul's Cathedral in November 2004, to form a pedestrian gateway into the newly redeveloped Paternoster Square. The gate was originally adorned with four royal statues (Charles I, Charles II, James I and Anne of Denmark) carved by John Bushnell and these have now been restored and returned to the four niches on the main elevations. The gate's name derives from the fact that it once stood next to the Temple law courts. A bar is first mentioned in 1293, at which time it was probably no more than a chain between wooden posts, but the term survives in this ancient Inns of Court. Although a relic from beyond the precincts of the City Wall, it is the only surviving example of London's City Gates.

'Ludegate, Newegate, Aldersgate, Crepelgate, Bisshopesgate, Alegate' and others enumerated in the City ordinances of 1311 were ordered to be closed at night at the beginning of curfew being rung at St Martin's Le Grand, and the pedestrian gates, or wickets, opened. These were then to be closed at the last stroke of curfew and could only be re-opened by order of the Mayor or Aldermen. 'The reality of Old London, walled and guarded', was brought back to Walter G. Bell on reading these ordinances pertaining to the Warder of the gate at Ludgate:

> That you, together with two men of the watch, well and fittingly armed, be at all hours of the day ready at the gate, within or without, down below, to make answer to such persons as shall come on great horses, or with arms, to enter the city; and that you set a guard above the gate, upon the leads thereof, to look out, that so may be the better warned when any men at arms approach the gate, And if any do approach in manner aforesaid, then let the chain be drawn up without, and answer be given in this manner: 'Lordlings, the King has given charge to us that no person shall enter his city by force of arms, if he have not special warranty from him. Wherefore, sirs, we pray you that you will not take this amiss; but as for you persons, you who are upon your palfreys, and you folks who come without bringing great horses or arms, you may enter, as being peaceful folks. And if they will not thereupon turn, then let the portcullis be let down by those of your people above, that so those other persons may in no way enter'.

Throughout the sixteenth century the City Gates acted more as police barriers than military defences. But still they were opened and closed according to ancient rule and did serve as a constant warning to threats of armed invasion or dangerous rebellion. In 1517 twelve riotous apprentices had been hanged and quartered, and their sad remains set up in all parts of the City as a warning to others. 'At the City Gates,' writes an eyewitness in 1518, 'one sees nothing but gibbets and the quarters of these wretches, so that it is horrible to pass near them.' After Wat Tyler's Rebellion the gates bristled with heads. In 1569 the Revolt of the Northern Earls to depose Queen Elizabeth I caused the City Gates and portcullises to be repaired, guns got into readiness and stocks of powder and shot distributed. The City Livery Companies were ordered to provide soldiers 'well and sufficientlie furnyshed with a jerkyn, and a pair of gally sloppes of broadclothe, collar watchet, one calyver with flaske and tuchebox, a moryan, a sworde and a dagger.'

In the Georgian era, the growth in shipping and trade between London and the New World was putting a severe strain on moorings. Between 1720 and 1800 trade tripled, and at times nearly 2000 ships were fighting for 500 moorings. Goods had to languish on the Thames sometimes for weeks. Access in and out of the City was hampered by the gates that once served to protect it. By 1799 all were removed. An announcement in the public journals of 1760 concerning the destruction of three of the gates on 30 July was made simply to the effect that a Mr Blagden, a carpenter of Coleman Street, gave £91 for the old materials of Cripplegate, £148 for Ludgate and £177 10s for Aldgate on the undertaking to have all the rubbish removed by the end of September. Only Newgate remained for a further twenty years until rioters put an end to it. Passing through London on his *Tour Through the Whole Island of Great Britain* (1724–27), Daniel Defoe makes

5 Photograph of Temple Bar

mention of Temple Bar as 'the only gate which is erected at the extent of the city liberties, and this was occasioned by some needful ceremonies at the proclaiming of any King or Queen of England, at which time the gates are shut; the Herald at Arms knocks hard at the door, the sheriffs of the city call back, asking who is there? Then the herald answers, "I come to proclaim," &, according to the name of the Prince who is to succeed to the Crown, and repeating the titles of Great Britain, France and Ireland, &. at which the sheriffs open, and bid them welcome, and so they go on to the Exchange, where they make the last proclamation.' As well as the statues of the four royals set below Temple Gate, so were there 'traytors above, the heads of several criminals executed for treason being set up there.'

On 10 November 2004, Alderman Robert Finch, Lord Mayor, officially returned Temple Bar to the City of London. Accompanied by the Sheriffs and Members of the Court of Common Council, he unveiled a plaque before being helped by fourteen of the stonemasons who worked on the project to officially push open the gates, each weighing just over a ton. The Lord Mayor declared that the bar was a symbol of London's history together with its modern role and hoped that it would act as a symbol of the City's welcome to the world for centuries to come. As the returned Temple Bar epitomises the disposition of the City of London, so do the remains of its Wall, its soul. Thus, following its route either in the physical or metaphorical sense, so it embraces all that is this Square Mile forged from a primeval forest that has evolved into the most vibrant and dynamic haunt of driven humans on the face of planet earth.

PART TWO

Walking London Wall
An Armchair Ramble

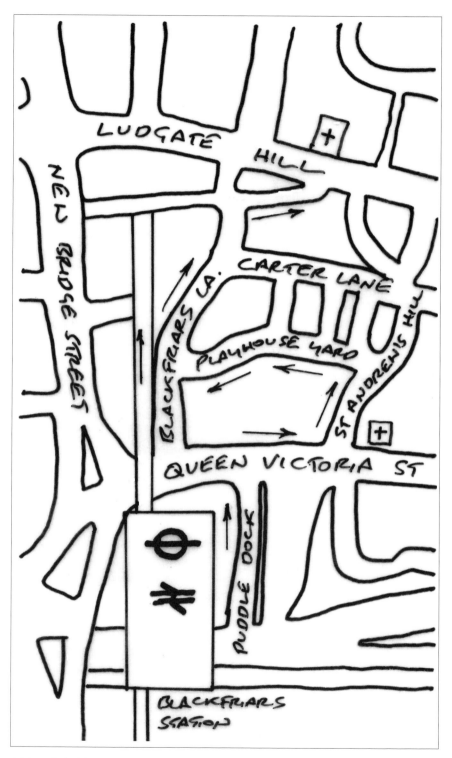

6 Map of Blackfriars to Ludgate Hill

Blackfriars to Ludgate

Finagle's Law of Dynamic Negatives (also known as Murphy's, or Sod's, Law) dictates that if there is more than one possible outcome of a task in hand then we are invariably left with the one that will result in an undesirable consequence. For no sooner were the opening words to this chapter laid down than it was announced that Blackfriars Station, used by around 44,000 City workers and tourists every day, will close from March 2009 until late 2011 to provide for a new upgraded station with increased capacity and better interchange facilities between the tube and national rail services. During this period the District and Circle Line underground services will not stop at the station and customers are advised to use 'nearby' Temple and Mansion House stations. Blackfriars mainline station will remain open while the £350 million project goes ahead to make it the first railway station in London to span the Thames.

That said, this is no bad thing. At the time of writing, Blackfriars underground station presents to the London Wall explorer not only an especially unpleasurable introduction, but a baffling multiple choice of exits from a warren of grim tunnels fanning out in all directions. Mercifully, the route to this adventure begins with a simple right turn on leaving the ticket barrier and up the steps for Queen Victoria Street. First impressions are not good here either. It is not a pretty aspect, with little in the way of grace or charm and even less in character, except that is for The Black Friar, a wedge-shaped public house to the left, resting its head against the railway bridge on the north side of the road. Built in 1875, it takes its name and inspiration from the thirteenth-century Dominican priory, which gives this area its name. Like the exterior, the interior of the building is as unusual as it is pleasing. Decorated like a cathedral, almost every inch is covered in marble, mosaic or bas-relief sculpture. Begun in 1904, with eminent sculptors and artists of the day contributing to its splendour, poet laureate Sir John Betjeman led a campaign to save it from demolition in the 1960s. The rest of Queen Victoria Street was not so fortunate; thus it represents the skin of much post-war City of

London landscape, but by no means its soul. Turning right (east), past Blackfriars National Rail Station, enclosed in its own especially lacklustre box, we arrive at the now unrealistically named Puddle Dock. A glimpse of the River Thames and the painted concrete wall of the Mermaid Theatre across the road complete the points of interest in this dim and dismal quarter. From now until the works are complete, it will be a matter of taking the tube as far as Temple Station and walking the extra 600 yards east towards Blackfriars Bridge and there taking the underpass to Queen Victoria Street and Puddle Dock.

Somewhere between no 1 Puddle Dock and Blackfriars Passage lie deep underground fragments of the western tip of London Wall that in Roman times dipped its toe into the River Thames. Looking back towards Queen Victoria Street, the whole of the north side is dominated (at the time of writing) by the pink candy-striped expanse of the Bank of New York Mellon Centre. I hesitate to offer a name because of the impermanence of companies in the City and where they set up business over time. The address, should this business up stakes in the near future, is 160 Queen Victoria Street, although quoting street numbers can also be a hazardous business. From the perspective of Puddle Dock, the centre of the glazed atrium of this building represents the line of the Roman Wall built 150 years after the foundation of Londinium. It would have stood about 20ft high, or equivalent to the underbelly of the building bridging the Puddle Dock traffic way. The sentry walk below the battlements would have been some 14.5ft from the ground, or about the height of the wall lamps offering a glimmer of respite in the gloomy underpass. As outlined earlier, the Wall basically consisted of two outer skins of coursed Kent ragstone, filled with a rubble and mortar core layered with flat red tiles or bricks at intervals for added strength and stability. In the fourth century, the Wall was strengthened with towers and a riverside defence was added. When the Romans left, the Saxons are said to have set up their own centre of occupation less than a mile to the west of this spot, during which time it is believed the Wall, and much of London, decayed. Successive repairs and restorations after the Norman Conquest heightened the Wall along its 2-mile run and more bastions were added, all except for this quarter where the Wall was swept away.

After his Coronation, King William I remained in London for some time organising his government. William of Poitiers praises the king's justice and clemency, instructing officials not to oppress the citizens of London. The *Anglo-Saxon Chronicle*, however, claims that heavy taxation was imposed, although the same record has the people paying tribute to King William that were free to buy land. Nevertheless William left London while key fortifications were completed to contain the restlessness of its 'vast and savage population'. These new defences comprised the White Tower at the east end of the City Wall and another here at the west end, known as Baynard's Castle after Bairnardus or Baynard, a Norman who accompanied the Conqueror in 1066. There would be two castles bearing the name of Baynard built in this quarter. The first stood behind 160 Queen Victoria Street and south of Ludgate Hill where another, lesser fortification called Montfichet's Tower was also built close to the banks of the River Fleet.

Both utilised the solid Roman Wall and ditch running parallel with the Fleet as their western boundary. The twelfth-century historian, Gervasius Tilbury, records these 'two most strong castles...built with Walls and Ramparts'.

In the year 1111 William Baynard succeeded to the property, but then lost his barony of Dunmow as a result of a felony he had committed. King Henry I granted it and the castle to Robert FitzRichard, the son of Gilbert, Earl of Clare and to his heirs. A century or so later Baynard's Castle and Montfichet's Tower were held by Robert Fitzwater. Having overcome the small difficulties with the king around the time of Magna Carta in 1215, the rebellious Baron was restored to favour together with all his holdings. Sixty years later he succeeded in enlarging the physical precinct of the City of London for the first and last time by means of a licence obtained from Edward I, to convey his property hereabouts to the Archbishop of Canterbury, for the foundation of a house and church for the Dominican Order of the Black Friars. As the Elizabethan historian John Stow tells us, it was in 1282 that work began to demolish that part of the Roman Wall from Ludgate to the Thames. The ditch was filled in and the Roman Wall demolished. Its replacement extended west to the River Fleet (now New Bridge Street) and a quay was built for the monks onto the Thames. In 1310 Edward II ordered the Lord Mayor and the citizens of London to finish the new City enclosure.

The major redevelopment of the Fleet valley between Holborn and Blackfriars in the 1980s and '90s opened up one of the largest single archaeological excavations ever undertaken in the City of London. The Fleet Valley Project, headed by archaeologist Bill McCann, ran from 1988 to 1992 and included the demolition of the railway viaduct over Ludgate Hill, and the construction of the new underground station and railway lines between Blackfriars and Newgate.

More than 80m of the medieval wall that surrounded Blackfriars was uncovered along New Bridge Street and Pilgrim Street. Well preserved and with a foundation width of 3m and an overall height of 3.5m in places, the medieval construction comprised stone from the original Roman wall demolished to make way for the Dominican priory. Masonry from St Paul's destroyed by fire in 1087 was also found to have been used.

The stretch of Wall between Ludgate Hill and the former east bank of the Fleet River was particularly well preserved, although one section had a very large vertical crack extending from top to bottom, which, for reasons of Health and Safety, almost put a halt on further archaeological investigation. 'The possibility of a substantial piece of masonry collapsing and causing a major accident was not to be contemplated,' recalls McCann, 'and the decision was taken to remove this section of the wall before the archaeologists were allowed into the area.'

The Wall, however, almost as if the Romans had built it, resisted all attempts over a two-day period to bring it down and the investigations were allowed to proceed. Eventually, what remained succumbed to the heaviest machinery and was laboriously removed stone by stone. As far as the original Wall from Ludgate to Puddle Dock is concerned, very little was found. There have been a number of excavations and watching briefs in the area, but no trace of the original Wall has

7 Photograph of Fleet Valley Project, Pilgrim Street looking west. *Courtesy of Bill McCann*

8 Photograph of Fleet Valley Project, South face. *Courtesy of Bill McCann*

9 Photograph of Fleet Valley Project, Pilgrim Street looking south. *Courtesy of Bill McCann*

yet been identified. 'The Times building south of Playhouse Yard will certainly have removed any survival and there seems as if the construction of the Friary may have done likewise,' concluded Bill McCann.

In 1806 a carved head somewhat less than life-size was found, thought to be part of a standing figure that once stood in a round-topped recess, above which was an inscription. A report read to the Society of Antiquaries from Charles Roach Smith in 1843 described it and other finds made at Blackfriars in the course of digging sewers. The memorial, dated AD 212–17 is dedicated 'To the spirits of the departed and Gaius Valerius Celsus, son of Lucius, soldier and speculator of the Second Augustan Legion'. The memorial was placed by Celsus' comrades, 'Atoninus Dardanus, Valerius Pudens and [?]....Probus, *speculatores* of the legion'. Depending on the school of thought, *speculatores* were scouts, look-outs or spies, or again a form of military police attached to the general staff. It now sits in the Museum of London along with the relatively few other relics discovered along the course of London Wall. Vestiges of the Black Friars church were also uncovered during the excavations of 1843 and what was thought a piece of the Roman Wall. Queen Victoria Street was created when the tunnel for the District Line Underground train service was dug between Westminster and Mansion House in the mid-nineteenth century. Blackfriars mainline station was built a decade or so after the Underground, completing the destruction, or burying what little might have remained of the Roman City Wall.

Like all of the City of London's major thoroughfares it is wise to cross where a pedestrian crossing is provided. This can incur inconvenient deviations from the line of enquiry, but better that than something more serious. The closest crossing to that of the line of the Wall here is that opposite 160 Queen Victoria Street where there is the choice of circumnavigating the building either to the left for Blackfriars Lane running parallel with the railway line, not a particularly pleasing route, or right for the meandering St Andrew's Hill with its historic buildings and pubs. St Andrew's Hill also follows the alignment of Castle Baynard's eastern defence, which took the form of a bank or ditch. There are also some of the City's finest eighteenth-century town houses surviving here. Either in 1612 or 1613, William Shakespeare purchased a house nearby. Whether the Elizabethan playwright actually lived here is doubtful. It's generally considered that he left London before 1611 and went back to his native Stratford where he spent the remainder of his days. On his death in 1616 the house passed to his daughter, Susannah Hall. He most certainly would not recognise the neighbourhood today, nor the high Victorian confection in the form of the Cockpit Inn, of which he was shareholder, but the cellar formerly belonging to a Priory Gatehouse was already three centuries old in his day.

Today the narrow valley disappearing left of the Cockpit Inn is called Ireland Yard, which leads into the former ecclesiastical enclave of the Black Friars. Facing us in the thirteenth century would have been the east end of their church, a large imposing structure more like a small cathedral. To the right, bristling little Burgon Street would have led to the Chapter House, the kitchen and cloisters. After the imaginatively named Friar Street there is Church Entry, which contains part of the churchyard of the former Church of St Anne Blackfriars, which was destroyed along with what remained of the monastery in the Great Fire of 1666. The church stood on part of the priory preaching nave, the choir on the other side, indicating the usual passage between the nave and chancel passing north and south beneath the steeple. The nave had seven bays and measured 114ft × 60ft. Following the dissolution in 1536 this part of the priory was used as a churchyard for the parish of St Anne Blackfriars. The other side of the churchyard faces onto Ireland Yard where, immediately right of the steps leading into is an exposed a fragment of rubble wall. On first glance it screams Roman, and looks to all intents and purposes like Kentish ragstone bonded in the same, solid manner as the City Wall. But the alignment is wrong. It is built east to west, not north to south, and, besides, it is a good 50ft from the line of the Roman Wall. In one of the offices behind it there is said to be a fourteenth-century monastery window protected by a sheet of plate glass, perhaps associated with this fragment.

On the day I went to photograph the artefact, most of the area was boarded up and taped off for yet more redevelopment work. I couldn't find the relic, and none of the workmen I asked remembered seeing 'any bit of old wall'. One of them, however, interested in what I was doing, kindly allowed me inside the ribbons of plastic tape to 'sniff around'. I had become confused with the two parts of St Anne's churchyard and was looking in vain at that part in Church Entry. It was then that the site foreman found me and I explained to him what I was looking for. After a while he took me round to the right part of the churchyard and pointed to a blue painted box constructed to protect the remnant. Such are

10 Photograph of rubble Wall, St Anne's Church, Blackfriars

the perils of sightseeing in the City; demolition and redevelopment works are constant companions. The City fathers had decreed a viewing grill be cut into the face of the protective woodwork, although a torch would have been welcome. Like me, the foreman was disappointed that we were not looking at an 1800 year-old piece of London history, but then again 800 years or so wasn't bad. And he reckoned if he had been around at the time he would have probably reused the stone from the Roman Wall to build the new development.

Ireland Yard gives way to Playhouse Yard, the site of the Priory's Upper Frater, or refectory, where Parliament met in 1311, the State Record Office was maintained from 1322 to 1323, and a court sat in 1529 to hear King Henry VIII's divorce case against Catherine of Aragon. The unusual width of Playhouse Yard allows a turning circle for carriages, as this was once the site of the Blackfriars Playhouse. James Burbage purchased the Upper Frater for conversion into a public playhouse in 1596 but sadly died before the works were finished. By 1608 a thirteenth share comprised part of William Shakespeare's local property portfolio and it was here that his King's Players performed. A musical interlude between acts was necessary because unlike the Globe and Rose theatres in Southwark, the Blackfriars Playhouse was enclosed and suitable for all-weather performances. Because it was lit by candles, the doors had to be opened regularly to avoid the suffocation of both actors and audience. It was demolished in 1655 and the site later gave way to the King's Printing House, where *The Times* newspaper set up business in 1785. The clock set into the building's tympanum later became the paper's famous masthead.

Contrasting the candy-striped backside of the Bank of New York's Mellon Centre, the more human scale of Georgian London is retained in the form of the buildings that line the north side of Playhouse Yard. When John Strype published his *Survey of London* in 1720, the sites of Baynard Castle with 'that of Mount Fitchet, near adjoyning' were timber yards, wood wharfs and private buildings. A round tower, thought to have been part of Baynard's Castle, was found incorporated in a domestic development, and two more were found as part of other buildings during construction in the nineteenth century. It is intriguing to note the bastion-like protuberance to the rear of Euromoney House, a former Georgian townhouse, including perhaps one of these references. As far as is known, there is no archaeological or documentary record other than Strype's observations to draw any real conclusions. Although much remodelled, the building clearly dates from the eighteenth century. Its foundations could echo something more ancient, as there is adjoining a mostly plain brick wall of much more modern construction, although sympathetically built to blend with it and its neighbour, another older building, probably early to mid-nineteenth century. Where they join, there is a small triangular kink off the yard on the line of the Roman Wall. The height of the first-floor windows can be used to gauge the height of the Wall, and the obtuse corner of this building is a suggestion of its width. About where the Queen Anne style doorway looks across the yard would have run the Roman ditch.

Today a dull stretch of grey painted hoarding offends the eye on leaving Playhouse Yard, forming the west side of Blackfriars Lane and hiding the railway line serving Blackfriars Station. The Fleet Valley Project concluded that between the Roman period and the middle of the eleventh century, this area between the City Wall and the Fleet river was apparently abandoned, and may have been used for cultivation, which is consistent with what is known of the Saxon period in the London area, where the major settlement was to the west of the Fleet, until the full reoccupation of the walled city during the upheavals of the Viking period. Apart from the possible light agricultural activity on this east bank of the Fleet, the only major feature at this south end dated to the Saxon period, was a communal grave dug into the foreshore at the confluence of the Fleet and Thames. Come the Black Friars and much of this bank was taken into the fold of the newly revised City Wall as far as the Fleet river, itself now given way to New Bridge Street.

The Priory's western cloister range constructed here was purchased in 1632 by the Worshipful Society of Apothecaries, one of the 107 City of London trades and craft associations known as Guilds or Livery Companies. The term 'livery' refers to the uniform of each guild, the latter deriving from the Saxon word for payment. From medieval times until the middle of the nineteenth century, liverymen had to be Freemen of the City in order to provide a degree of control over their activities in the form of trading standards, quality control and working conditions. As these City companies grew and prospered, so they acquired their own halls to meet, settle disputes, discuss business and socialise. Of the few medieval halls that survived the Great Fire of London in 1666, all have perished at the hands of rebuilders or German bombs during the Second World War. Several of the thirty-eight halls in existence today were rebuilt on original medieval sites. Apothecaries Hall dates from its reconstruction following the Great Fire. The external appearance has altered little since the late eighteenth century. The interior in the form of the Great Hall, the panelled Court Room and Parlour remains as it was when the hall was rebuilt between 1668 and 1670. And while the south and rear sides in Playhouse Yard create a pleasing contrast to post-war austerity, it is the front of this building that really lifts the spirit with its ornate central doorway set into a cream semi-stucco façade. It's not open to the public, but the courtyard doors are often open for a peek into a rare and altogether different world.

Continuing north to the top of Blackfriars Lane is the junction with Ludgate Broadway and Carter Lane, where a blue plaque on a wall to the right marks generally the 'Site of the Priory of the Blackfriars founded 1278', but unspecifically the site of its main gatehouse which stood here. Carter Lane was once the main east to west thoroughfare when the original cathedral church of St Paul's was enclosed in its own wall. The name of the lane derives from two Carter Brothers shown as taxpayers in Castle Baynard Ward in 1319. A few yards along to the right is Carter Court, a narrow passage leading to a tiny enclave of modern offices built in the Georgian style. The passage itself is lined with what looks like a poorly executed wood finish covered in a thick layer of lime wash. However, this is wattle and daub and the wooden planks hammered in with crude iron nails are sole survivors from the sixteenth century. Indeed, this is reputed to be the only built structure between the Monument and the Temple to have survived the Great Fire of 1666.

As Carter Lane echoes the southern boundary to Montfichet's Tower, so does the slight meander of Ludgate Broadway its western boundary in the run of the Roman Wall. First recorded in 1136 as either 'Mount Fitchet' or 'Mountfiquit's Castle', the round fortified tower was built by Norman nobleman William Montfichet. Like that of his near neighbour, Robert Fitzwalter, his descendant at the time of King John, Richard Montfichet, was one of the rebellious Barons who challenged the king and was banished to France in 1213. Likewise his property, including the castle on the bank of the Fleet, was confiscated. On his return to England he doesn't appear to have been interested in restoring it. In a charter dated 10 June 1276, the Mayor of London, Gregory de Rockesley, together with the Barons of London, granted Robert Kilwarby, Archbishop of Canterbury 'two Lanes or Ways, lying next to the Street of Baynard's Castle, and the Tower of Mountfiquit, or Mountfichet, to be destroyed.' The Investigator to the Society of Antiquaries of London, F. Cottrill, writing in 1937, mentions a piece of Roman wall found at 56, Carter Lane (now Ryan's Bar) which seems to have been similar in thickness and construction to the City Wall and had been used as evidence for a south-easterly course in this neighbourhood. Archaeological work undertaken by the Museum of London between 1986 and 1990 at 1–3 Ludgate Square and 56–66 Carter Lane established the site of the Norman fortress, truncated rubbish and cesspits of unknown date, a fragment of medieval cellar wall foundation and infilled post-medieval well, but nothing of the Roman Wall. One of the tentative conclusions to emerge from The Fleet Valley project is that a mill and its associated pond, owned by the Knights Templars, halted the completion of the revised City Wall until the order was finally suppressed in the early fourteenth century, when 'the turret' (Montfichet's Tower) demanded by Edward II was completed at the point of the former mill pond. The name Montfichet is immortalised today in an office building on Ludgate Hill, once the Tower's north ditch. The eastern boundary after the thirteenth century formed part of a cemetery just north of Carter Lane where the several notables interred included the parents of Catherine Parr, the last of Henry VIII's wives.

Ludgate Broadway gives way to Pilgrim Street where the remains of the medieval extension to the City Wall stood 10ft above the contemporary ground level in 1882. Heading east along Pilgrim Street is to skirt the southern end of Ludgate, the first City Gate on this clockwise perambulation of London's Wall. Entering Ludgate Hill the church of St Martin-within-Ludgate sits opposite. To the right and up the hill is the iconic aspect of St Paul's west façade, the third version of the cathedral since AD 604 to occupy this low plateau sloping south to the Thames foreshore and west to the banks of the River Fleet. The medieval cathedral destroyed in the Great Fire dwarfed Wren's 365ft-high dome and cross with its 489ft spire. As well as St Paul's, St Martin-within-Ludgate is one of the fifty-two City churches rebuilt after the Great Fire of 1666 under the direction of Sir Christopher Wren. Aptly dedicated to a patron saint of travellers, it sat next to Ludgate as the first and last building on entering or exiting the City. During the Roman period Ludgate Hill continued as part of the *via decumana*, or the main east–west passage through Londinium. It would almost certainly have been lined with buildings before the first gate was constructed around AD 200 as part of the City's defences comprising a wall, external ditch and internal bank. The findings of the Fleet Valley Project question some of the assumptions previously made about the City Gate at this point. The alignment of the Roman road and even its natural gradient was reduced in the later Roman period from a precipitous 1 in 10 to a calmer 1 in 20. The new road surface consisted of crushed ragstone laid on a thick layer of fire debris. The street was also widened and the height of the Fleet Bridge raised by 9ft.

The Roman origin of Ludgate built into this Wall was also archaeologically demonstrated for the first time. Evidence from the excavated remains of Roman road surfaces suggest that Ludgate Hill was originally 11m wide and that Ludgate itself began as a double gate. The northern half was blocked in the medieval period, probably by the initial construction of the church of St Martin next to it. Excavations at Newgate in 1904 showed the City Gate at that point in the Roman period was identical to Ludgate. Another piece of the medieval Wall was visible in the late 1930s as the rear support to nos 41–43 Ludgate Hill. There appears to be no trace surviving today, not even in the shop numbers. The best guess is that the remains lie underground somewhere between 39 and 45, opposite Ye Olde London public house on the north side of Ludgate Hill, which stands on the northern half of the original Roman gate, later dubbed Ludgate.

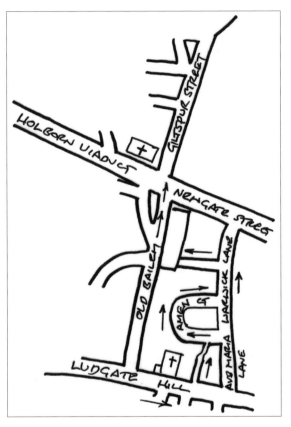

11 Map of Ludgate to Newgate, 2008

2

Ludgate to Newgate

Ludgate Hill is the western of the two hills upon which the Roman settlement of Londinium was founded. Before the demolition of Ludgate, (the gate itself), in 1760, this City thoroughfare was effectively split between that part of the hill leading up from the River Fleet, known as Ludgate Hill, and that inside the City Wall, which was called Ludgate Street. The blue plaque on the wall of St Martin-within-Ludgate should by rights be attaching to Ye Olde London public house where the City Gate actually stood. The romantics of the past have had it that the first gate was erected here in 66 BC by Lud, a legendary king of the Britons, as the entrance to a town he built during his reign which was protected with huge towers around its city walls. It was called Caerlud, meaning in his native Welsh tongue, 'Castle of Lud', which the Romans subsequently dubbed Londinium. An alternative version has it that when he died, he was buried near the gateway later named in his honour by the Saxons. A corruption of 'flood gate' is another theory. Today, as all too often happens, that which bore his name for over a century has been renamed. His likeness, cast in bronze above each entrance door of the one-time Ludgate Circus landmark, is joined by the same stylised face looking down from lead panels dated 1992 when presumably the pub was curiously re-christened 'Leon'. Way back in prehistory, this spot would have represented a small island, or eyot, of high ground in the swampy banks of the Fleet. Another formed the other side of today's Ludgate Hill, and together they had an inestimable influence on the subsequent development of this part of London.

The demonstration of these two high spots was another fascinating element of the Fleet Valley Project, showing that the Romans made use of both outcrops during the first and second centuries AD, the northern island supporting a large milling complex and the southern a small timber jetty and a large warehouse possibly associated with the mill. At the end of the second century AD the regression in tide levels in southern Britain reduced the value of these eyots and perhaps saw the first Roman bridge built across the Fleet founded on masonry piers, one of which used the southern eyot as a solid support. This may well have coincided with that other major civil engineering project around AD 195–225, the enclosure of Londinium within a massive Wall. After the decline of the Roman occupation around AD 450, the old walled City appears to have been abandoned in favour of a Saxon settlement known as Ludenvic further west towards the modern day Strand. The nature and extent of settlement in this area are largely unknown until after King Alfred refounded London within the walled City during the ninth century. Either shortly before or shortly after the Norman Conquest in 1066 a major new bridge was constructed spanning the Fleet at Ludgate, the massive timbers of which formed part of the abutment on this east bank found in the excavations of the two eyots. A minor tributary of the Thames flowing from Highgate and Hampstead, Camden's *Brittania*, the first published topographical survey of the whole British Isles, records the 'Fleete' as 'a little riveret (whence Fleetestreete tooke name), now of no account but in times past able to beare vesseles, as I have read in the parliament Rolls, sheddeth itselfe into the Tamis.' Sir Christopher Wren's plans for rebuilding the City after the Great Fire included grand wharves and quays along this stretch of the Fleet, but he only managed to build a new bridge over the river at Holborn in 1674 when this final section of the waterway was deepened and canalised. It is its pollution since the fifteenth century, however, that has made it legendary. Jonathan Swift in *A Description of a City Shower*, published in 1710, describes the state of the river: 'Now from all parts the swelling Kennels flow, And bear their Trophies with them as they go: Filth of all Hues and Odours seem to tell What Street they sail'd from, by their Sight and Smell.'

In 1732, the Fleet was arched over from Holborn Bridge to the Punch Tavern in Fleet Street. Thirty years later and the section to the Thames was similarly covered, reducing it completely to a sewer. Today it discharges into the Thames under Blackfriars Bridge where a campaign is underway to have a viewing platform erected to view this mysterious watercourse taste freedom. Meanwhile, there is a small iron grill set in the service road along the New Bridge Street side of The Black Friar pub. At the time of writing this is the last spot where it's possible to see flow of the Fleet before its outflow into the Thames. There is a neat round hole cut beneath the grill, but a torch proves a vital piece of kit.

Ludgate Hill remains a very busy route in and out of the City, so crossing the line of the Wall for Ye Olde London and St Martin's church London is a matter of personal choice. There are concrete bollards in the middle of the road in the direction of Ludgate Circus. Using them and then turning back up the Hill towards St Paul's is to pass Old Bailey, a name referring to the early defensive outwork, or bailey, outside the City Wall, but now more familiar as the colloquial term used for the Central Criminal Court. Along its length was first the V-shaped ditch cut by the Romans, some distance from the natural watery defence of the Fleet Valley.

Ye Olde London public house occupies the spot that in Roman times was the north side of the double gate into the City Wall. The pub's only claim to fame, however, is that it boasts that rarest of all attractions in a City of London pub, a beer garden. Reached from the basement bar, this tiny open space represents one of the few publicly accessible spots on the route of the Wall. Excavations by the Post Office in the 1920s showed the natural ground at Ludgate to be some 10ft below the modern street level, or about half that of this diminutive open space, offering a natural light source for the benefit of the pub and neighbouring offices. The towering east wall is that of St Martin-within-Ludgate. In 1790, a fire took hold at the nearby premises of Messrs Kay, which uncovered some thirteenth-century remains of the Wall and other discoveries have been made in St Martin's Court behind the church. When he was rebuilding it, Sir Christopher Wren discovered a monument to a soldier carrying a rod in his right hand, possibly signifying some kind of office, and a scroll in his left hand. In 1806 fragments of Roman monuments were found nearby and the remains of a bastion at the back of the London Coffee House, precursor to Ye Olde London. These remains projected 4ft from the line of the Wall into the City Ditch and measured 22ft from top to bottom. The stones comprising it were of different sizes, the largest and the cornerstones rudely squared. So strongly built was it, bonded together with cement of hot lime, that iron wedges had to be driven in to break the stones apart. There were also small square holes in the sides of the tower that were used either to hold timber floor joists or as sentry spyholes. The adjacent part of the City Wall was about 8ft thick and described as being of 'rude workmanship', consisting of irregular-sized stones, chalk, and flint. The bricks found, perhaps the only clues to Roman work, were on the south side, bounding Stonecutters' Alley. The base of this circular tower stood about 3ft below the pavement where some remains of Roman art were found. An etching made in 1807 includes an inscribed hexagonal pedestal base in memory of Claudia Martina, aged nineteen years. A badly damaged carved stone female head found with it is thought to have belonged to the same monument, and a dowel hole on the pedestal indicates that it supported a figure, probably a portrait statue. The pedestal capping is carved with rolls in the tradition of altar tombs and the lettering dates it to about AD 100. That it was found as part of the masonry near the remains of a circular staircase suggests it was taken from the nearby cemetery when the bastion was built. The effigy of the Roman soldier and the monument to Claudia Martina now rest in the Museum of London.

In its own meagre nod to history, Ye Olde London's beer garden boasts an odd display of nineteenth-century tombstones that appear to have no obvious local connection. There is also a lump of stone that looks as though it might have been worked. The day I dropped in, there were three Eastern European girls on duty who knew nothing about the contents of the garden. In fact, it is closed until lunchtime on weekdays but they let me go and see it anyway. One of them took an interest and asked, echoing my American friend, 'Why you knock everything down in London?' I told her it was a long story and instead described how the girth of the Wall would have filled the entire area of the beer garden, reaching up half as high as the walls about us on its way north towards the Old Bailey. 'I go there,' she beamed, 'to see the crimes.' I told her there was a large lump of Wall deep in the bowels of the courthouse. She laughed as though what I said was really funny.

12 Illustration of Medieval Tower discovered south of Ludgate Hill, 1792

King John was excommunicated in a dispute over the appointment of the Archbishop of Canterbury in 1209. He had used this as an excuse to confiscate church property and sell it back to his bishops at a profit, using part to fund his continental ventures, which did not have the support of his Barons. A number of them rebelled in May 1215, choosing as their leader, Robert Fitzwalter, custodian of nearby Baynard's Castle. While attempts to take Northampton Castle were met with failure, the Barons passed peacefully into London through Ludgate on 17 May, prompted in part by Fitzwalter's base close by. Other versions have it that the citizens opened Aldgate to them and another that the Fitzwalter's men scaled the City Walls at a time when most of the inhabitants were occupied at divine service, opened the different gates in succession and made their way in. Clearly recognising the importance of the City's primary defence system, Stow records: 'Robert Fitzwalter, and Geoffrey de Magna villa, Earl of Essex, and the Earl of

Gloucester, chief Leaders of the Army, applyed all Diligence to repair the Gates and Walls of this City, with the Stones of the Jews broken Houses. Especially (as it seemeth) they then repaired (or rather Builded) Ludgate.' A stone found embedded in the gate was engraved in Hebrew characters: 'This is the ward of Rabbi Moses, the son of the honourable Rabbi Isaac'. Following protracted negotiations between King John and the Barons, a deal was agreed at Runnymede in June 1215, which contained provisions designed to curb the king's exploitation of loopholes in feudal custom and confirm people's rights under Common Law. For the first time in Britain's history the king was subject to the law of the land and it is the only clause that remains on the statute books to this day. The agreement was, however, only ever seen by King John as a temporary measure intended to demonstrate his reasonableness. It probably meant little more to the rebels either. That they reneged on their agreement to surrender London demonstrates their disdain. Essentially, Magna Carta was doomed to failure and lasted less than three months. By November 1215, King John had recaptured Rochester Castle and was poised to strike at London. The rebels had offered the crown of England to Prince Louis of France. Instead of taking London, King John began ravaging the rebels' homelands, giving Louis time to muster an army. For a moment in time the fate of Britain hung in the balance. If King John failed, England would have fallen into French hands. Yet in an incredible twist of fate he died, leading the way for his son, who as King Henry III, reissued Magna Carta and shifted the conflict from a civil conflict over baronial rights to a successful war of resistance against foreign invasion.

In 1260, Lud Gate was 'Repaired and Beautified with Images of Lud, and other Kings' and by 1378 had become one of three separate sites for the Ludgate Free Debtors' Prison. The rooms above it were used to house the more refined class of criminal such as Freemen of the City and clergy who had been imprisoned for debt, trespass and contempt of court. For treason and other serious criminal offences there was Newgate Gaol a quarter of a mile to the north. John Strype notes that the prisoners in Lud Gate Gaol were chiefly merchants and tradesmen brought down by losses at sea. It was enlarged in 1463 by the widow of Stephen Forster, a fishmonger who became Lord Mayor of London in 1454. In his younger days, so it is said, Forster had found himself a prisoner in Lud Gate and while at the begging gate a rich widow took pity on him and paid the £20 he owed to secure his release. She took him into her service and eventually they married. A successful businessman when he died, Forster's widow ensured that his wishes for improved conditions at Ludgate were carried out. Provision was made for an open-air 'walking-place' on the south-east side measuring 38ft×29ft. There were prisoners' rooms above it with a leaden roof and, 'for the easement of prisoners', there was to be free lodging and water. As much as was inscribed on a copper plate set up on the wall of the new quadrant:

> Devout Souls that pass this way,
> For Stephen Forster, late Maior,
> heartily pray,
> And Dame Agnes his Spouse,

to God consecrate,
That of Pity, this House made
for Londoners in Ludgate.
So that for Lodging and Water,
Prisoners here nought pay,
As their Keepers shall all answer
at dreadful Dooms-day.

This episode provides the foundation of William Rowley's proto-typical Jacobean City comedy *A Woman Never Vext*, wherein Mrs Forster asks her husband why the prisoners are removed from Ludgate. He replies: 'To take the prison down and build it new, with leads to walk on, chambers large and fair; For when myself lay there the noxious air choked up my spirits. None but a captive's wife can know what captives feel.'

A tower was added to the gate in 1463 to increase the capacity of the gaol. The stone, bearing the plaque and Forster's arms of three broad arrowheads that was fixed over the entry to the prison, was preserved by John Stow when the gate was rebuilt. In the reign of Edward VI (1547–1553) the fanatical zeal of the citizens of London against anything approaching idolatry resulted in the decapitation of 'Lud and his family' adorning the gate. When King Philip came to London after his marriage to Mary in 1554, thirty prisoners in Ludgate, who owed a staggering £10,000, presented the king with a Latin speech written by the distinguished classicist and toxophile, Roger Ascham, who begged the king to redress their miseries, and by his royal generosity to free them, 'inasmuch as the place was not a dungeon for the wicked, but a place of detention for the wretched'. Philip ignored the plea while Queen Mary, who was said to be 'partial to all images,' had the broken figures of King Lud and his sons repaired.

Twenty-eight years into the reign of Elizabeth I Ludgate was again 'sore decayed'. It was pulled down in 1586 and rebuilt at a cost of £1500, complete with the figures of King Lud and others on the east side. The 'picture of the lion-hearted queen' on the west is thought to be the only image of the virgin Queen carved in her lifetime. On completion of the rebuilding, the court ordered that signs on houses at the western end of St Paul's churchyard were to be taken down and rehung below their lower jetty, presumably to improve the view of the gate. Thanks to Marmaduke Johnson, a poor Ludgate debtor in 1650, we are left with a vivid impression of conditions in seventeenth-century Ludgate: 'The officials in King Lud's House,' he begins, 'included a reader of Divine service, an upper-steward called the master of the box, an under-steward, seven assistants (one for each day of the week), a running assistant, two churchwardens, a scavenger, a chamberlain, a runner and six criers at the grate who by turns kept up the ceaseless call to passers-by to "Remember the poor prisoners!"' Corruption was rife. The officers' charge for taking a debtor to Ludgate was between 3 and 5*s*, although the due amount was just 2*d* for entering the name and address and 14*d* to the turnkey. Lodging was between 1 and 3*d*. Sheets were 18*d*, although 'chamber-fellows' paid 4*s*. Non-payment saw the confiscation of the prisoner's clothes, or 'mobbing,' as it was called, until he did pay. Sixteen pence was also payable to one of the stewards for what was called 'table money'. On discharge there was a Master's fee of 2*s* to pay, 14*d* for the turning of the key and 12*d* for every infringement of the rules. For leave to go out with a keeper, prisoners paid a security for the first time of 4*s* and 10*d*, and 2*s* on every subsequent occasion. These exorbitant fees swallowed up all the prison bequests, which meant that inmates had to rely on 'means from the Lord Mayor's table, the light bread seized by the clerk of the markets, and presents of under-sized and illegal fish from the water-bailiffs'. A handbill dated 1664, containing the petition of 180 poor Ludgate inmates, was used by prison alms-seekers who walked the streets with baskets on their backs and a sealed money box in their hands. 'We most humbly beseech you,' states the handbill, 'even for God's cause, to relieve us with your charitable benevolence, and to put into this bearer's box — the same being sealed with the house seal, as it is figured upon this petition.'

Destroyed in the Great Fire of 1666, Ludgate was substantially renovated and 'beautifully repaired', although the lot of the prisoners appears to have altered little. *Prison Thoughts*, published in 1682 by Thomas Browning, a citizen and cook of London and a prisoner in Ludgate, described a place 'where poor citizens are confined and starve amidst copies of their freedom'. A writer in the *Spectator* newspaper reported that 'passing under Lud Gate the other day, I heard a voice bawling for charity which I thought I had heard somewhere before. Coming near to the grate, the prisoner called me by my name, and desired I would throw something into the box.' Describing the gate in 1720, Strype confirms that on the east side, that is the side facing St Paul's Cathedral, the three niches containing the carved effigies

13 Illustration of Ludgate burning in the Great Fire of London 1666

of King Lud and his two Sons remained. And on the west facing the timber bridge that spanned the River Fleet, was Queen Elizabeth I, complete with the Arms of England and France above her. As well as a breach in the City Wall at this point, Strype points to several other minor gates and posterns (pedestrian gates) 'built for the convenience of Passage into and out of the City'. In 1760, the year of George III's accession, London's City Gates were seen as an impediment to traffic and therefore to trade and were ordered to be taken down. Ludgate was demolished in that year and the materials sold for £148. The prisoners were removed to the London Workhouse and eventually transferred to a new debtor's facility near Newgate. The royal effigies of King Lud, described as being 'of very rude workmanship', were destined to end their days in 'the parish bone-house' until they eventually found sanctuary in the church of St Dunstan-in-the-West, Fleet Street, together with the statue of Queen Elizabeth I where they remain to this day.

There has been a church on the site of St Martin-within-Ludgate since 1138 or 1174. The first rebuild was in 1437. After the Reformation, the patronage of the church shifted from the Bishop of Westminster to the Bishop of London and then to the Chapter of St Paul's where it remains. William Penn, whose son founded Pennsylvania was married here in 1643, twenty-three years before it was destroyed by the Great Fire. Rebuilding was not completed until 1703 when it was set back from its old site with the widening of Ludgate Hill. Another major rebuilding and alteration took place in 1894, raising the floor level at the east end and creating the chancel area. During the Second World War, St Martin's received the least amount of damage of all the City churches, suffering only some minor harm to its roof in 1941 caused by an incendiary bomb. In 1954 St Martin's became a Guild church; that is one without a parish but with other responsibilities and functions. The pulpit is original to the church, dating from 1680, as is the decorative screen behind the altar. There is also a set of seventeenth-century bread shelves that came from St Mary Magdalene, Old Fish Street. After morning service, bread given by more wealthy parishioners would be placed on these shelves for the poor of the parish to collect.

Stationer's Court is located on the left past the church. Yet another discrete passageway snaking its way through the City interior, it opens out onto the new site purchased by the Stationers Company for their Livery Hall in 1611. Completed in 1677, Stationers Hall was constructed on the site of Lord Abergavenny's house, formerly known as Brittany and then Pembroke's Inn. During modernisation in the early 1800s, when it was given its striking new façade by Scottish architect Robert Mylne, Roman remains were discovered in the garden, including parts of Roman and Medieval Wall and gateway, as well as the tower, or bastion, described earlier. These remains had been left in situ, probably after the Great Fire as a foundation for new buildings, or indeed later walls. There is a gate immediately to the left on entering this attractive little square offering a balanced mixture of old and new, and it gives a glimpse of the soaring wall running from the rear of St Martin's church. Enclosed by another wall to the right is the garden belonging to the Worshipful Company of Stationers and Newspaper Makers, dominated by an enormous plane tree allegedly marking the spot where heretical books, condemned by the ecclesiastical authorities, were burnt in Tudor times. The old Company of London Stationers was incorporated in 1557 and enjoyed, until the Copyright Act of 1842, the sole right of having registered at their offices every pamphlet, book, and ballad published in the kingdom. Although no longer compulsory, the practice of entering books at Stationers Hall is still used for copyright purposes. The register rolls of books entered here represent an invaluable resource to literary historians.

At the north-east corner of the square, past the splendid new wing added to Stationers Hall in 1887 is a neat passage representing possibly the smallest business car park in the land, which leads out to Amen Corner. To the left of this slender corridor is the south access to Amen Court, a tiny township of exquisitely preserved seventeenth-century houses built for the Canons of St Paul's, a short distance from Paternoster Row, which was where the monks finished their Pater Noster (a Christian prayer) on Corpus Christi Day before processing to the cathedral. When they reached the corner, or bottom of the Row, they said 'Amen'. Then turning down Ave Maria Lane they chanted their Hail Mary's before crossing Ludgate, where they chanted the Credo. The high wall, glimpsed through the gate in Stationer's Court, now looms larger and more foreboding at the rear of Amen Court and the temptation is to march in for a closer look. But alas there is a notice written large in white letters on a blackboard cautioning that permission is required before entry, as this is a private court belonging to the Chapter of St Paul's Cathedral. But all is not lost. At the bottom of Amen Corner is Warwick Lane where a left turn leads north towards the rear of the Central Criminal Court. A matter of yards to the left along this otherwise unremarkable modern thoroughfare is a highly ornate red brick anomaly with the year 1880 carved atop its Tudorbethan gable. This is the gatehouse to Amen Court, complementing entirely the miniature scene beyond of bygone domesticity. The same cautionary notice as that posted in Amen Corner preserves the privacy of the residents. Respecting this, but the daylight being such that I had to get a photograph of the massive wall seen quite clearly from here, I nudged just inside what would have passed for the portcullis housing had the building been several centuries older. 'Yes?' enquired a voice almost immediately the moment I approached the arch. I explained to the emerging figure exactly what I was doing, or rather what I wanted to do. He carried a hand radio, like half a dozen or so others in Warwick Lane, busily checking large delivery vehicles to ensure the security of the law court. They all wear the bright yellow vests emblematic of such public work, unlike my interrogator who wore a suit.

He told me he had 'covered' a number of the London ghost walks at this location and wondered if I knew about the 'Black Dog of Newgate', a canine spectre sometimes seen on the top of the wall, or of the terrible stench said to stretch back to a time when famine struck London and starvation forced the felons in Newgate into cannibalism. One large man imprisoned for sorcery was devoured in a matter of days. I admitted I didn't know this, only that The Justice Hall, or The Sessions House, formerly stood on the other side of the wall. Built in 1539, its positioning between the City of London and Westminster provided

14 Photograph of Sessions House Wall, Amen Court

a suitable location for trials involving people from all over the metropolis north of the River Thames. The medieval courthouse was destroyed in the Great Fire and rebuilt in 1673 as a stately three-storey Italianate brick building. In front of the courthouse was the Sessions House Yard, a place where litigants, witnesses, and court personnel could gather, separated from the street by a brick wall with spikes on top to prevent the prisoners from escaping. In 1737 the building was remodelled, and enclosed. It was then that the forlorn passageway was constructed linking the courthouse with the dreaded Newgate Prison close by. This wall shielded the journey of condemned prisoners led to their executions, who were later buried beneath it. 'Dead Mans Walk', as it is known, survives on the other side of the wall, hence its place on the City ghost tours. The colossal wall dates from the days of the Old Sessions House and Newgate prison, demolished in 1902. My contribution to the conversation was clearly not as interesting, but I was allowed entry to take a closer look at the wall nevertheless.

To call the Session House Wall impressive is something of an understatement and it offers an excellent idea of life inside and beside the old walled City. In March 2000 the Museum of London carried out an evaluation of nos. 7–11, Old Bailey prior to demolition. One trench was positioned so as to coincide with the external face of the City Wall. Modern brick and concrete rubble was found to a depth of about 3m beneath a modern yard. This was found to form the backfill of a brick walled structure with a stone-flagged floor. As the Sessions House did not have basements, this was thought to be part of a substantial ventilation channel leading from beneath the centre of the building to an air shaft at the rear, which existed before 1890. A trial excavation beneath the floor of this channel revealed a glazed, ceramic sewer pipe and a small area of apparently in-situ archaeology comprising ragstone cobbles. Engineering constraints meant that most of the trench did not go below 13m. The backfill was only fully removed at the southern end of the pit and although the available inspection area at this depth was small, it appears that the ventilation channel had removed all traces of the superstructure of the City Wall. Where some of the Roman make-up deposits and foundations did survive they were not disturbed by drains and sewerage. A number of architectural and worked stone artefacts dot the area of Amen Court, especially a profusion of what look like ragstone blocks around areas of planting. All these relics are clearly survivors of much earlier times, as are the houses themselves enjoying a brief view of the sky above the wall before the new edifice rises.

A few yards north of Amen Court is Warwick Square, said to have been the site of a London house belonging to the Earl of Warwick and now dominated on two sides by the Central Criminal Court. During the building of the New Sessions House in 1903 a 76ft length of London Wall was exposed with evidence of a fifteenth-century archway thought to have provided direct access from Warwick's house into Old Bailey. In 1547 what is described as the Inn of the Earl of Warwick was being used as a storehouse for the King's Revels. In charge of it was John Brydges, Yeoman of The Revels and Merchant Taylor. He was summoned before the Court of Aldermen to answer for damage done to the City Wall by allowing rain to fall onto it from his roof. Unfortunately all of the Wall uncovered in 1903 failed to share the same veneration and was destroyed. About here filtered air was drawn into the underground ventilation chambers by means of an enormous fan, received in a large chamber in the roof of the old court. Thereafter it was discharged by means of a gigantic iron cowl 15ft in diameter and weighing two tons through the subterranean air tunnels knocked through the old City Wall. A tiny gated open space featuring a stone pillared arbour occupies the mouth of Warwick Passage at the south-west corner of Warwick Square. A marble plaque on the wall explains that these pillars were taken from the Lord Mayor's entrance to the Old Bailey and demolished in 1969 prior to the building of the new wing hich was opened in 1972. Between this comparatively recent addition and its new emerging neighbour can just be glimpsed the end of the high wall running out of Amen Court. Taking its line into the court buildings is to imagine a reasonable chunk of the Roman City Wall preserved in the basement as a Scheduled Ancient Monument. Discovered in 1900 to the rear of no 8 Old Bailey beneath the premises of the Oxford University Press, it measures over 8ft high and as much again thick and stands today as one wall of the basement. For security reasons it's not possible to visit this first substantial relic of London Wall.

In 1834 the name and jurisdiction of the Old Bailey changed, reflecting the growth of London beyond the City of London and Middlesex to include parts of neighbouring counties. The addition to the Central Criminal Court, built in the 1970s, increased the four original courtrooms to nineteen and at the same time gave evidence that London Wall cannot have been built earlier than AD 190 and also that its construction was begun from the south-east corner, the most

15 Photograph of Roman Wall exposed on the site of Newgate Prison, 1903

vulnerable stretch. That part from Bishopsgate to Cripplegate enjoyed the natural protection of the boggy moors, and the stretch from Newgate to Blackfriars the same, courtesy of the River Fleet. Dating evidence was found when an internal turret of the Roman City Wall was discovered, which contained an accumulation of Roman rubbish on the gravel floor in one corner beneath the stairway. A coin forger had usefully dumped a handful of coins and two coin moulds for casting imitation bronze and silver coins. The bronze coins comprised two of Antonius Pius (AD 145–61) and one of Commodus (AD 180–92). The silver denarius was

16 Photograph of Roman Wall in the basement of Central Criminal Court, Old Bailey

of Caracalla, the eldest son of Septimus Severus, and Roman Emperor from AD 211–217, which was dated AD 213–17. Another coin of Commodus, dated AD 183–4 and found in the thickening of the Roman fort at Cripplegate indicates that the Wall cannot have been built earlier than AD 190 and that it was completed between then and AD 220, a period of about 30 years.

Warwick Passage leads to Old Bailey and the relatively bland façade of the new extension. Further north is the more famous face of E.W. Mountford's building, considered one of the best examples of neo-English Baroque architecture in London, crowned by the iconic domed cupola supporting Pomeroy's figure of Justice reaching a height of 212ft. Old Bailey ends at the junction with Holborn Viaduct, Giltspur Street and Newgate Street, the latter crossed conveniently at a set of traffic lights opposite the gloriously impressive Viaduct Tavern. Opened in 1869 along with Holborn Viaduct, the world's first flyover connecting Holborn with Newgate Street over the Fleet Valley, this striking Victorian pub has a large curved frontage with many of its original features intact, including paintings, gilded mirrors and fine examples of decorated glass. At the back of the bar is a beautifully carved manager's booth complete with intricately engraved glass panels. The ornate ceiling is made from beaten copper and supported by cast iron pillars. Best of all, however, are its cellars, former cells of the notorious Newgate Gaol no less, which can be toured by appointment. Meanwhile, on the wall of the Central Criminal Court opposite is a blue plaque declaring 'The Site of Newgate demolished in 1777'. This does not allude to the prison, but to the site of the City Gate from which the infamous institution took its name.

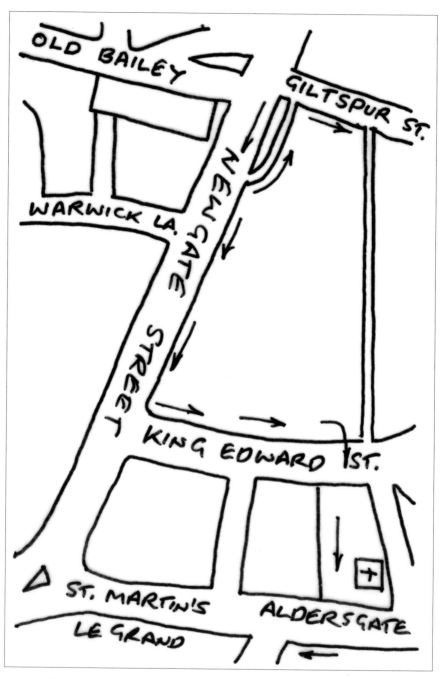

17 Map of Newgate to Aldersgate

3

Newgate to Aldersgate

In September 1903 an important section of the Roman Wall was found during excavation of the site of Newgate Prison, in some parts about twelve feet high. William Lethaby saw it in October of that year, noting a foundation raft of rubble in clay finished with a layer of concrete, then a course of plinth stones on the outside. A course of roughly square facing stones was laid onto a thick bed of mortar and then another thick line of mortar running down between the stones as grout. Between this and the next four courses came the tile bonding which, except for the three courses behind the plinth stones, carried right through the thickness of the wall. The tiles were regular Roman bricks about 18in long by 12in wide and 1.5in thick, laid to Flemish bond. The stone facing courses were a little higher at the bottom, but all were comparatively small and square and with a clear distinction between them and the unworked rubble filling, which was essentially concrete. Some remnants of the Roman gate were also revealed. In fact, archaeological discoveries at Newgate offer the only hard evidence as to what the Roman gates looked like, the most significant being a portion of plinth found on the City side, with a return at the south end. When linked to earlier discoveries made in 1875, it was possible to draw up a plan of the gate. The plinth had been removed from where it was found before Lethaby saw it, but he was able to confirm that the stones were definitely Roman with a chamfer 3in wide and a square face of similar width below. They had been strongly cramped together and one had a return end that clearly came from a corner. A portion of the western plinth discovered later in 1909 showed that the gate, with its towers on either side, had a frontage of about 96ft. The space between the towers was about 35ft, sufficient for two large archways much like the great gate at Colchester, which measured about 107ft wide and had two carriageways 17ft wide and two small side openings 6ft wide. At Newgate, enough of the adjacent Wall was found in 1875 to show that it was constructed of stone bonded with tiles. The gate itself was erected on a thick platform of clay and ragstone finished with a layer of concrete. This raised the Gate plinth about 5ft above that of the adjoining City Wall, leading Norman Cook to believe that the gate was built some time after the Wall had been completed. An accumulation of rubbish about 5ft over the Wall plinth suggested to him that the roadway at this point was that much above the ground level when the gate was built. He casts no doubt, however, on the gate's Roman provenance, its plan exactly that according to type with a double roadway between square flanking towers projecting within the Wall 18ft on the north side and 8ft on the south side.

Excavations in the late 1980s and early '90s indicate that the gate was first constructed about AD 200, although this prime western route linking Londinium with Silchester and Gloucester is thought to date much earlier, to around AD 55. Other archaeological finds have included a rare statue of the Roman goddess Minerva and a Roman cemetery to the south predating the Wall. A late second-century building, thought to be a Romano-Celtic temple, situated just outside the City limits overlooking the Fleet, was replaced by an early fourth-century masonry building with heated rooms. The Fleet Valley Project uncovered evidence of a series of third-century glass kilns north of Ludgate Hill which pre-dated the octagonal temple, described by Bill McCann as 'a very large and prestigious building, the largest yet to be found in Britain and comparable to many of the major sites in Gaul'. It was built around AD 270 and seems to have remained in use for upwards of fifty years before it was destroyed, perhaps by fire or possibly it coincided with the period when Christianity had become well established in Britain. The replacement building was equally large and of an altogether different character, a multi-roomed building with ragstone walls and *opus signinum* floors (a simple type of patterned pavement mosaic) that underwent at least three conversions, one of which included the addition of the hypocaust system. The full extent of the building was not seen in the excavations but clearly it was of some importance. It may have functioned as a mansio (coaching house, or official stopping place), 'its situation immediately outside and between the two City Gates at Ludgate and Newgate make this an attractive interpretation', suggests McCann.

Presumably the Roman gateway, or at least parts of it, survived reasonably intact for almost 1000 years if Stow is correct in telling us that a New Gate was erected during either the reign of Henry I (1100–1135) or of King Stephen (1135–1154). This rebuilding followed the fire that destroyed the cathedral church of St Paul in 1086, little more than a century since the old Minster had been ransacked by the Vikings in 962. Then Mauritius, the Bishop of London, embarked on an ambitious project to create an impressive architectural statement in the style of the Normans, never before seen in Britain. After Mauritius, Bishop Richard Beaumore continued the work, going on to purchase the streets and lanes around and about the cathedral, increasing the church territory within a 'strong Wall of Stone and Gates', which impacted on the passage from Aldgate in the East to Ludgate in the West. Thus an early form of congestion bypass was created north of St Paul's, along Cheapside for the wooden bridge spanning the Fleet. As far back as the time of King John (1199–1216) the New Gate attaching the scheme was used as a gaol. Like Ludgate it first catered for 'Felons and Trespassers' more than the hardened criminal. In the year 1218, Henry III wrote to the Sheriffs of London, commanding them to repair the gaol for the safe keeping of his prisoners. The Calendar of the Liberate Rolls (Royal Charters) record an order by this same sovereign in 1236 directing the Mayor and Sheriffs to pay Gerard Bat and Robert Hardel a sum of just under £100 to construct a prison in one of Newgate's turrets, less 100m the King contributed himself. In his *Dictionary of London* (1918) Henry A. Harben refers to a manuscript dated 1285, which mentions 'Chamberlain's Gate', possibly alluding to William the Chamberlain of London who is recorded in the Domesday Book as having a vineyard close by in Holeburn (Holborn). By this time the institution was already being referred to as an 'Heynhouse' or 'hateful gaol.' Its ongoing maintenance and repair and the costs of opening and closing it were met by an order of Edward II who granted the Mayor the proceeds of a year's merchandise entering the city devoted towards its upkeep. It was nearly destroyed in 1381 when Wat Tyler's Kentish rebels attacked it and released the prisoners, 'thus adding them to the hordes of rascality which then were sacking the town'.

Unlike neighbouring Ludgate, Newgate began to cater for more than the mild transgressor. Among the new order were 'naughty Women' who murdered their illegitimate children, often by throwing them into 'Houses of Office' (a common name for a toilet). So 'horribly loathsome' had conditions become at Newgate that a licence to renovate the festering establishment was granted to the executors of Richard (Dick) Whittington in 1422, bringing about the underworld tag thereafter of 'Whittington's College', or simply 'The Whit'. Originally in the Parish of St Sepulchre, Holborn, Newgate was transferred to the new parish of Christchurch when the old Greyfriars Monastery buildings became the home of Christ's Hospital. The words of the Indenture dated 27 December, 1547, convey Henry Vlll's grant 'And all the tithes, and offerings of the inhabitants of all the houses and buildings in the said gate called Newgate of London, and of all the inhabitants within the same gate called Newgate now being parcel of the parish of St Sepulchre without Newgate aforesaid.'

As the Common Gaol for the County of Middlesex, Newgate was damaged by fire in 1555. Repairs to the east side were begun in 1630 by Sir James Campbell, the Mayor of London, and finished the following year by his successor, Sir Robert Drury against a backdrop of discontent between King Charles I and Parliament. The subsequent heavy financial burden falling on the citizens of London led to a reaction in favour of the king, which in April 1648 saw the apprentices' rise, seize Ludgate and Newgate, and attack the Lord Mayor's house. A message was sent to Lord Fairfax, whose troops eventually restored order. For six weeks the chains removed from the City streets were replaced by order of Parliament or assent from the City. Towards the end of May, all gates and posterns were closed and guarded while the City was searched for 'disaffected persons'. On 29 May 1648 the City finally decided to stand by Parliament and its gates became passageways once more.

At least with regard to Newgate, the Great Fire of 1666 proved a bonus in so far as the old edifice could be rebuilt much stronger and fit for purpose. Completed in 1672 with two posterns for pedestrians and a main passage for road traffic, its embellishments included the statues of Liberty, Peace, Plenty and Concord. But alas more fire damage occasioned its periodic repair and rebuilding, culminating in its final form in 1679, incorporating more ornamentation and emblematic figures including that of Dick Whittington and his cat. Inside, however, conditions were as appalling as ever. The water supply was inadequate, the stench was overwhelming with no ventilation and disease was rife. In 1716, after the failure of the first Jacobite Rising, Newgate's already particularly crowded population was swelled with rebels. On the evening of 4 May that same year the Warder was attacked in the exercise yard and his keys seized. Headed by Brigadier Mackintosh and his son, around seventeen of the inmates overpowered the turnkey on duty and escaped. Four ran east towards Cheapside. Mackintosh and two others boldly walked out of the City through Newgate itself, duping the guards and making for the River Fleet where they boarded a ship for France and freedom.

With its violence and corruption, Newgate was described by Henry Fielding as a 'prototype of hell'. It was eventually pulled down and a new gaol erected between 1770–78 when the City Gate was finally removed. The new building, now the site of the Central Criminal Court, enclosed three internal courtyards and was variously described as 'very large, strong and beautiful' with the 'most consistent and terrifying display of rusticated stone in English architecture.' Nevertheless its status as a symbol of cruelty and oppression persisted. Soon after its completion it was attacked by the mob during the Gordon Riots, allowing the prisoners to escape. It was rebuilt ten years later, involving substantial clearance of a large area alongside the building. Old Bailey until then was divided into two parts, 'Old Baly' and 'Little Old Baly', separated by a triangle of buildings. The place of public execution was at Tyburn, some 6 miles west. A merchant tailor called Robert Dow, who died in 1612, appointed the Sexton of neighbouring St Sepulchre's-without-Newgate 'to pronounce solemnly two Exhortations to the Persons condemned: For which, and for Ringing the Passing Bell for them as they are carried in the Cart by the said Church, he left 26s 8d yearly for ever'. The Admonition to be pronounced to the condemned criminals, as they passed by St Sepulchre's church called on 'All good People pray heartily unto God for these poor Sinners, who are now going to their Death, for whom this great Bell doth Toll.' In 1783 the place of public execution was eventually moved to the natural arena still evident today at the junction of Newgate Street and Old Bailey. Executions were removed to the interior of the building in 1868 and marked thereafter by the flying of a black flag and the slow tolling of the bell.

Newgate was the last of the City Gates to be pulled down, authorised by the Act of 1767. The blue plaque in the wall of the Central Criminal Court marks not only the location of the gate but also the run of the City Wall. To follow it from here requires stepping out of history and into the new millennium in all its splendour, courtesy of the 52,000 sqm Merrill Lynch Financial Centre.

A public route is provided via the tiny alley next to no 115 Newgate Street, one of a parade of preserved Victorian shops and offices. The contrast with what lies within is breathtaking. Capable of employing in excess of 4500 personnel, this stone, brick and glass micro-city includes restaurants, a gymnasium and television studio, client centre with 28 meeting rooms, a roof garden and a number of green spaces and a glazed galleria running east–west through the vast site. As well as the restoration of the listed buildings integrated into the complex it was a requirement of the designers to make the scheduled remains of the City Wall available for public viewing.

On a brick wall just before the Giltspur Street access point there is a smart bronze plaque which reads: 'The remains of the Roman and medieval City Wall and Newgate are located beneath this site. The position of the Roman wall is marked by the textured paving in this passage and the main courtyard'. In that courtyard is another plaque proclaiming: 'The remains of the Roman City Wall, constructed around AD 200, and a medieval bastion, are preserved in a chamber beneath this building.' The entrance to that chamber is at the north end of the Merrill Lynch building in Giltspur Street by Security Gate 1. Here another plaque bears the welcome news that the remains below can be visited by the public, subject to prior booking. The day I arrived – unannounced – I did ask if I could see the remains without an appointment and was despatched to main reception. There I was re-routed to a door marked Staff Registration where inside a large number of smart Merrill Lynch employees were waiting to be, well, registered. My instinct told me that I was in the wrong place and mentioned as much to a senior security officer passing by. He thought that there was a telephone number on the information plaque by the security gate, but after radioing through to his colleagues discovered there was not. 'Are you from the council?' he asked, looking at my clipboard. I denied the charge and told him the reason for my interest and asked if many people came to see the remains. 'Yes', he replied, 'a lot.' How the tourist or the casual visitor managed to arrange it, he wasn't sure. 'Wait there a moment, would you please,' he asked politely before disappearing back into the Staff Registration office. When he reappeared it was with a colleague who was detailed to take me to see the remains and furnish me with all the information I might need. How nice, I thought, genuine customer service.

Frank Cottrill, the then Investigator to the Society of Antiquaries writing in 1937, declared the remains of the Bastion and Wall at Giltspur Street to be the 'most remarkable feature of the whole course – the great re-entrant angle formed by the wall at the northwest, turning south.' Walter G. Bell at the same time explained how funds were allotted for preserving these 'massive remains' in the concrete chamber built in 1909. Then, as today, members of the public were allowed access, but then only on written request to the Secretary of the General Post Office on whose property it was. Walter Bell hoped that one day this restriction would be lifted and that the public would be able to visit it at will. 'Modern science' provided frames of prismatic glass overhead to bend the daylight onto the face of the Wall and the first instance found in London of

the rounded angle example bastion. Bell declared the state of preservation to
be 'remarkable' with stones 'of no mean size, still grey and white, in the lower
courses, above smaller stones, embedded in a hard mortar about a core of rubble
and above the rows of bonding tiles. The half sweep of the bastion was almost, but
not quite, complete. Worryingly, an inch or two of 'undesirable water' welled up
from the ground. And so it remained until the demolition of the vast Edwardian
Post Office enclave in 1999. A detailed photographic and fabric condition survey
was carried out by the Museum of London that revealed a portion of the bastion
had suffered from this watery intrusion resulting in some serious mortar loss.
Otherwise, apart from evidence of subsidence, the remains were found to be in
excellent condition. The holes within the external face were identified as those
used by the builders to take short pieces of timber (or putlocks) used to support
the floor of a scaffold. An excavation of nine of the eighteen shaft-like trenches
dug within the line of the Roman City Wall revealed that this area had little
more to offer in the way of any other Roman building activity. Instead it mostly
comprised pathways and backyards or external surfaces, although traces of clay
and timber buildings and one stone-built structure with a cellar were found.
Also discovered were rubbish pits dating from AD 50–70, which contained some
Samianware and amphorae.

One trench revealed evidence of burned-out mud brick buildings from
the same period that might represent Boudican destruction. As evidenced by
widespread rubbish pits and wells, by AD 70–90 this whole area was divided into
properties with parts of the site nearest to Newgate Street largely built over. Access
to the street was provided by a number of gravel paths or track ways. Several other
clay and timber buildings were destroyed in about AD 120–130 and replaced, but
overall, after the late second century, it seems the density of building declined,
as more of the area was used for the dumping of soil, rubbish, and pit digging.
Pottery found in the internal earthen bank dating from AD 160–250 indicated
that the area settled before the construction of the City Wall extended further
north. No sign of the first phase of the Roman City Ditch was discovered, but in
one trench a series of intercutting ditches of either late Roman (AD 270–400) or
Saxon-Norman date was found, as was evidence of the late Roman strengthening
of the internal earthen bank. Around AD 400 Roman settlement declined and
except for pit digging it appears the area was virtually abandoned. Pollen samples
confirm that it remained that way for 500 years until the presence of Saxon-
Norman cesspits and rubbish pits confirm that the Newgate Street frontage was
reoccupied. By the thirteenth century most of the area was built over and all
waste disposed of in stone lined pits, obliterating all traces of the earlier City
Ditch. By the early sixteenth century the ditch had become filled with soil and
rubbish. One account has it that this stretch was systematically filled in 1553, the
Agas map of London (1562) showing the area to be one mainly of backyards.
Up until the eighteenth century little more was revealed other than brick-built
cellars, wells, drains and cesspits. By 1787 the majority of the site was cleared of
buildings to make way for the Giltspur Street debtors' prison, built to house the

previous occupants of Ludgate, and in 1825 a large cellared hall was built over the infilled medieval City Ditch. Surveying the site in 1909, William Lethaby noted a rubbish pit measuring about 50ft×35ft, which in Roman times had been covered with concrete over a foot thick and where three buildings had been erected on the spot.

In the interests of Health & Safety, the 10ft journey below street level to see the remains can today be taken either by lift or a twin set of smart blue metal stairs. I took the stairs. Down at the Roman level is an ante-room with a map on the wall showing the vastness of the Post Office building where the last letter was sorted less than a century after the foundation stone was laid by King Edward VII in October 1905. Elsewhere within the foundations of the replacement financial complex are buried the tunnels and train tracks where mail was conveyed between the northern and southern divisions of this huge expanse. Now safe and secure in museum conditions, with proper lighting, the length of Wall and bastion resemble in shape a question mark, with the medieval bastion as the head and the Roman Wall the tail. Although viewed from a raised platform, this in no way diminishes their potency. The outer face of the bastion measures about 20ft in circumference and the fragment of Wall about half as long again. William Lethaby was here on 5 July 1909 when these remains were excavated. He noted that the section of Wall was badly fractured and inclined outwards, evidence of settlement problems according to the nature of the ground comprising predominantly wet clay on the bank of a stream. He also noted that the ground level is lower at this spot, with the foundations of the bastion sunk lower still. In keeping with all the other bastions, this one is not bonded to the Wall, but built against it, typically of a horseshoe shape and of thin courses of rubble. With regard to the inferior foundations and the problems of settlement over the 2-mile length of the Wall, Lethaby concludes that these bastions were built later, not only for their added defensive value but also to cover cracks and to act as buttress supports. In a sketch he made of the discovery at the time, the plinth and the foundations are seen in a corner of the bastion and below a sloping bank of wet clay leading to the pool of water that has since been diverted. Subject to Health & Safety warnings it is possible for the modern-day visitor to step down to the Roman level by moving around to the rear of the piece, 'careful of any sharp protrusion'. But the 'risk' is worth it. Standing inside the bastion is to experience the security afforded by this substantial fortification. It is also incredible to consider just how much this part of the planet has expanded in volume over the past 1900 years, with the foundations of these remains 20ft below the modern street level. Close up, the distinctive elements of Roman building techniques become more obvious, with the ubiquitous runs of red tile adding strength and robustness. On the dry gravel fronting of the Wall, where the subterranean watercourse once filtered through, is what at first glance appears to be a Roman plinth but is in fact one half of the Post Office building's west entrance doorstep. It's a nice idea to incorporate the different eras, with the medieval and the Edwardian each borrowing from the Roman.

18 Photograph of City Wall remains at Merrill Lynch HQ. © *Graham Gaunt*

19 Photograph of bastion remains at Merrill Lynch HQ. © *Graham Gaunt*

There is a service road running from Security Gate 1, which follows the route of the Wall, including three more bastions. The middle one was found to have no foundation extended outside the base of its walls and was not stepped into the Roman ditch. Instead it went straight down into the brick-earth below the plinth of the City Wall. No reused, carved or shaped stones were found in its core, and the only obvious Roman material was a quantity of tile fragments worked into the masonry. There was a second and wider ditch observed to the west of the bastion, but it lacked the expected character of the late Roman ditch, being V-shaped. The situation here was complicated by the presence of the small stream passing through the Wall at this point, which probably accounts both for the unusually deep foundations and for the bastion's solid base. One of these bastions was cleared away during the building of the General Post Office in 1906 and put through a stone-breaker to be used as ballast when paving the yard and the other was dynamited during construction work in 1936 with the rubble similarly used. There is no public access along this service road, which means backtracking to Newgate Street, either passing the Viaduct Tavern to inspect the Newgate dungeons, or returning via the Merrill Lynch passageway back into Newgate Street where another survivor of these recent improvements is the south façade of the old Post Office building. Gracing the central plinths of this imposing frontage are two blue plaques, the first commemorating the site of Christ's Hospital School, also known as the 'Bluecoat School' because of its distinctive blue uniform, which was founded in 1552 by Edward VI as a hospital for orphans. A school was later attached. The girls' school moved to Hertford in 1704 while the boys' remained, moving to Horsham, Sussex, in 1902 to allow for the building of the General Post Office building. Many of the buildings subsequently demolished once belonged to the former Greyfriars Monastery, recorded on the second plaque. These were rebuilt under Wren's supervision following the Great Fire, with Nicholas Hawksmoor completing the designs in 1696. The Franciscan Friary of Greyfriars occupied this site from 1225 until the dissolution of the monasteries by Henry VIII in 1538. It was founded by a handful of the Franciscan friars who landed in England from Assisi in 1224 and were given land between Newgate and the City Wall. The Friary prospered, supported both by royalty and by the City, including in 1421–5 money from Mayor Richard Whittington to build a library. After 1538, the tombs, including those of Queen Isabella and Joan, Queen of Scotland, were destroyed and the church renamed Christ Church.

At the junction of Newgate Street with King Edward Street stand the oldest remains on this immediate landscape in the form of Christ Church Greyfriars, dating from 1225. In size the church was second only to St Paul's Cathedral. The heart of Queen Eleanor, wife of Henry III, was buried here, and Margaret, the second Queen of Edward I, was interred before its high altar. The church burned down in the Great Fire and was rebuilt by Sir Christopher Wren who designed a new tower and choir, although the church was not rebuilt to its full size. Apart from the tower, all else was destroyed by enemy bombing during the Second World War. Today it is a public garden. Redevelopment permitting, it is sometimes possible to cut the corner of King Edward Street by turning left before Christ Church vestry (now a business unit) and taking the more picturesque Christian Passage alongside the thirteenth-century south-facing wall.

On the west side of King Edward Street is the even grander main entrance to the former General Post Office (or King Edward's) building, peppered and adorned with just about every classic architectural reference imaginable. Fittingly set before it is the statue of the father of the postal service, Rowland Hill. King Edward Street is named after the sovereign who founded Christ's Hospital, and not the one who laid the foundation stone to this monument of royal constancy, which reads: 'Edward the Seventh King of Great Britain and Ireland and the British dominions beyond the seas, Emperor of India laid this stone of King Edward's building of the General Post Office on the 16th day of October 1905 upon the site of Christ's Hospital founded in 1552 by King Edward VI'. This stately building ends at the service road running from Merrill Lynch Security Gate no 1 in Giltspur Street. A postern, or pedestrian gate, was 'made out of the Cities Wall' at this point to provide access between Christ's Church Hospital and the Hospital of Saint Bartholomew in Smithfield. License was given in 1553 to the Lord Mayor and Aldermen, to break down as much of the City Wall as required in creating the passage. When Christ's Hospital and St Bartholomew's Hospital passed into the hands of the City Corporation in 1582, a more substantial and turreted postern was built.

The red-brick gates on the other side of the road lead into another green haven, which follows the line of London Wall. Postman's Park, as it is called, is made up of the former churchyards of St Leonard's Foster Lane, St Botolph-without-Aldersgate and the graveyard of Christ Church Greyfriars Newgate Street. It opened as a public open space in 1880 and was enlarged by the addition of more land bordering Little Britain in 1883. The clue to the park's name is in the area's prime industry for more than a century, but is perhaps better known for the unique memorial it contains conceived by the painter and sculptor George Frederic Watts in 1887 to celebrate selfless men and women who sacrificed their lives to save others. Of the many commemorated on the Arts & Crafts tiles set into the sheltered wall is PC Greenoff who is remembered for saving the lives of many at a terrible explosion at Silvertown on 19 January 1917. Fitter's labourer, Thomas Griffin, died on 12 April 1899 in a boiler explosion at a Battersea sugar refinery when he was fatally scalded after attempting to save his mate. And a year earlier, seventeen-year-old Elizabeth Boxall of Bethnal Green was killed trying to save a child from the path of a runaway horse.

The buildings lining the southern boundary of the park represent the external face of the City Wall and the park itself the foul, reeking ditch. So offensive was it that in 1552 draper John Calthorpe paid for its arching over from Newgate to this point. At the same time on the other side of the Wall, the once broad ribbon of common land, measuring in all some 40 acres across the 2-mile length, was gradually being let out for gardens and houses or was sold. By the seventeenth century neither the Wall nor the Ditch retained much in the form of defensive value and were viewed more as obstructions and nuisances. At the east end of the park is the church of St Botolph-without-Aldersgate. Like St Martin, St Botolph is a patron saint of travellers, with blessings bestowed from a church on this spot for 1000 years. The current example was extensively rebuilt in 1627 and survived the Great Fire largely intact, sustaining only minor damage. There are a pair of very interesting column pedestals astride the entrance, finely carved and conceivably of an age much greater than the present church. There are also some intriguing chunks of stone set into the tower, possibly fragments of London Wall, or pieces from the City Gate that until its demolition in 1761 gave meaning to the church's suffix, 'without Aldersgate'.

According to John Stow, the name Aldersgate came about not after a great man, a builder or an unusual abundance of elder trees, but for the very antiquity of the City Gate itself, as in 'elder' or 'older'. Like Aldgate further east, Aldersgate is thought to have been one of the first four northern City Gates. In order to differentiate between these two venerable access points (so Stow has it) one was called Aldgate, and the other Aldersgate. When the Emperor Hadrian came to the imperial throne in AD 117, he decided that the Empire needed securing, not expanding. Thus, around AD 120 Londinium was afforded a stone fort, which occupied an area of about 12 acres, complete with a natural moat provided by the broad fens of Moorfields. It had a gate at each point of the compass built into walls complete with square turrets or watchtowers. By AD 200 the whole of Londinium was itself encircled within a stone wall that incorporated the west and north walls of the fort. A gate was built into the new City Wall immediately west of the fort, which eventually made its west gate redundant. That replacement gate became known as Aldersgate.

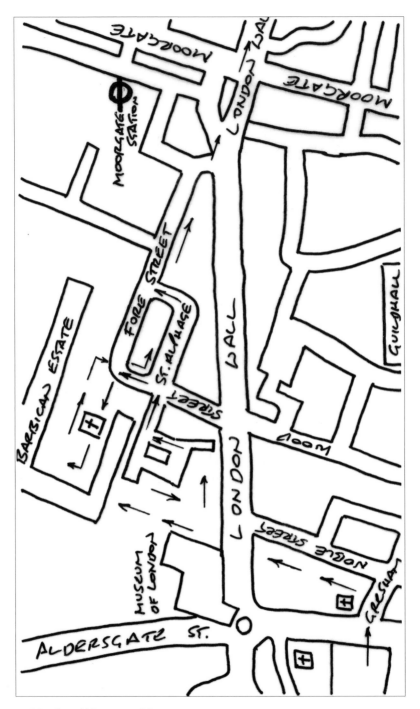

20 Map from Aldersgate to Moorgate

4

Aldersgate to Moorgate

Today there is a blue plaque on the wall of the Lord Raglan pub on the east side of the road marking the location of the gate that has subsequently given its name to this busy thoroughfare. Archaeological evidence hereabouts suggest a gate of late Roman military design with twin roadways flanked by semi-circular projecting towers built of solid masonry with an elevated platform for heavy weaponry such as catapults. In an article on the City Walls published in the *Journal of the London Society* (November 1922) Dr Norman reports the remains of an 'inner angle' bastion uncovered not far from the west end of neighbouring St Anne and St Agnes church. *The Great Chronicle of London*, however, written by Alderman Robert Fabyan, a Lancastrian who died in 1513, has it that Aldersgate was strengthened as a defensive work by a medieval barbican, built some 35ft in front of the City Wall, not behind it. These remains might relate to the death of Edward III in 1327, when the French were threatening the south coast and ordinances were issued for the safeguarding of the City. The gates fortified with portcullises and chains and 'barbykanes' were added. But by 1510 these defences were in a very poor state, 'in Joberdy of fallying downe, yt synks so sore'. Presumably repairs were effected by 1549 when the rooms above Aldersgate were occupied by the famous printer John Day (or Daye), who printed the folio Bible dedicated to Edward VI in 1549. In 1559 John Foxe came to England and was a guest of the Duke of Norfolk at Christchurch, Aldgate, and worked every Monday at Day's printing office, doubtless preparing the copy and reading the proofs of his *Book of Martyrs*. The first edition was issued in 1563, and the following year he took up residence with Day, remaining with him for the next seven years. John Day was the first printer to cut and use Anglo-Saxon type. He also produced very fine fonts of Italic, Roman, Greek and Music type. He issued the first Church Music Book in English in 1560 and in 1570, the first English edition of *Euclid*. Roger Ascham's *Schoolmaster* was another of his publications, as well as one of the earliest English Almanacs *A prognostication for the yeare of our Lord 1550*.

Stow tells us that Day 'builded much upon the Wall of the City'. So much so that the south side of the gate, that facing into the City, had attached to it a great timber-framed extension containing a number of large rooms and lodgings. On the east side, where the Lord Raglan public house stands today, was another huge timber extension with a large floor paved with stone or tile, complete with a deep well curbed with stone and rising into the room two stories high. Stow's source had never seen the like before in the whole of London. But despite these abuses, the Gate retained its defensive and law enforcement role. On 8 March 1579 the Watch at Aldersgate was drawn from the Haberdashers and Leathersellers Livery Company upon whom it fell to enforce Queen Elizabeth's Proclamation for the reformation of abuse of 'great hose, swords, daggers and other disorderly apparel.' This provided that 'no person shall wear any Sworde, Rapier, or suchlike weapon that shall pass the length of one yarde and half a quarter of the blade, at the uttermost; nor any dagger above the length of twelve inches in the blade at most; nor any buckler with any point or pike above two inches in length on pain of fine or forfeiture of weapon'. According to the City record, Lord William Howard, brother of the Earl of Surrey, attempted to pass through the gate wearing ruffles deemed to be 'much out of order'. Also one of his men carried a sword of forbidden length and with the point upwards. The Citizen guard, respectful of his Lordship's grand station, pointed out these infringements, at which point the servant carrying the offending sword drew the weapon to fight the guardians of the gate. Howard himself weighed in with an assortment of 'very odious names… which might have bred disorder of the citizens had they not been discreet men'. However, this being the third occasion whereby he had flouted the Queen's orders and threatened the citizens, the Lord Mayor requested the Lord Treasurer to take such steps to remedy the situation for fear the citizens might be discouraged from the task of safeguarding the City.

By the seventeenth century Aldersgate had become ruinous and was in danger of falling down. The Mayor, the Aldermen and the Common Council ordered its removal and rebuilding 'in a beautiful manner' to a design by one Gerald Chrismas. The cost of more than £1000 was found out of a legacy left for the purpose by William Parker, a merchant tailor. 'The taking down of the first tile' began on 31 March, 1617. The first stone was laid by the Right Worshipful, Sir William Craven, Knight and Alderman, on 26 May. Thereafter payments continued to be made in stages, the first when the building reached above 1yd high, the second when the gate was arched over and the third on completion. The job of 'Direction, Ordering and Overseeing' fell to a Mr Richard Fox, Citizen and Clothworker, described as a 'most painful, and industrious Person.' As to the exterior ornamentation, on the north side, in a large square over the arch, was the figure of King James I on Horseback, 'in the Posture as he came into England, entering the City through Aldersgate 'when', as Daniel Defoe described it, 'he arrived here from Scotland, to take the crown after the death of Queen Elizabeth'. Over his majesty's head were the quartered Arms of England, Scotland, and Ireland. On the east side was the Prophet Jeremiah, with the accompanying text: 'Then shall enter into the

Gates of this City, Kings and Princes, sitting upon the Throne of David, riding in Chariots, and on Horses, they and their Princes, the Men of Judah, and the Inhabitants of Jerusalem; and this City shall remain for ever'. On the west side was the figure of the Prophet Samuel with the text: 'And Samuel said unto all Israel, Behold, I have hearkened unto your Voice, in all that you said unto me, and have made a King over you.' On the south side was a bas-relief of King James I in his royal robes sitting in his Chair of State.

In common with Ludgate and Newgate, Aldersgate later doubled as a prison. As Daniel Defoe observed in a rather depressing echo of modern times: 'There are in London, and the far extended bounds, which I now call so, notwithstanding we are a nation of liberty, more publick and private prisons, and houses of confinement, than any city in Europe, perhaps as many as in all the capital cities of Europe put together.' The celebrated engraver William Fairthorne was a guest of His Majesty in 1660, the same year that Samuel Pepys recorded in his diary for 20 October: 'This afternoon going through London and calling at Crowe's the upholsterers in St Bartholomew's I saw the limbs of some of our new traytors set upon Aldersgate which was a sad sight to see; and a bloody week this and the last have been, there being ten hanged, drawn and quartered'. Six years later and Aldersgate was badly damaged in the Great Fire. So too was The Mourning Bush, a large neighbouring tavern, which revealed in its vaulted cellars remarkably fine early brick arch work and what was believed to have been the foundation wall of the Roman City Gate. More evidence of the Roman gate nearby was discovered in the 1890s in the form of a foundation for a bridge over the City Ditch, and almost a century earlier when clearing the site for another monumental Post Office building in 1818, workmen opened up two vaults that had served as cellars, one formerly the crypt of St Martin's Le Grande, demolished in 1547. Built in the fourteenth-century pointed style, it afterwards became the cellar of the Queen's Head. The second, a square vaulted chamber divided by piers 6ft sq and thought to have supported the nave, was of an even earlier date. A coin of Constantine was discovered and a stone coffin containing a skeleton. Lower down, Roman remains were found in abundance.

Described as 'heavy and inelegant', Aldersgate was soon repaired and improved after the Great Fire in the style of the other City Gates, with a central arch for general traffic and two arches either side for pedestrians. The City Crier was given the rooms above. Defoe noted that the unusually finely painted and gilded statue of King James was in pristine condition and that there were some emblematic figures remaining. Defoe also mentions another gate, a temporary affair, 'form'd for the day at the bars, where the liberties of the city end, that way which is now called Goswell Street' and which was taken down after the procession. Another witness to the life and times of Georgian London was the spectre of the omnipresent pauper. Situated as it was on the boundary line of a City parish, Aldersgate was very much the bugbear of eighteenth-century churchwardens. If, for example, a pauper woman had a child born in the parish, that child had secured a 'settlement' in the eye of the law, and was chargeable to the parish. Any expectant mother who was a stranger was not therefore welcomed. An entry in a Churchwarden's accounts for 1725 records such a woman 'big with child' laying up at the Bull and Mouth Inn, presumably about to produce. She was given 1s and the Watch at Aldersgate 6d for seeing her out of the parish. When the City Gates were torn down in 1761, Aldersgate was sold for £91.

Aldersgate is said to pre-date Bishopsgate, with evidence of a north–south aligned arterial road established by the second century AD found at 7–12 Aldersgate Street. But Bishopsgate has never been surveyed, so we don't know for sure. With regard to the Great North Road, opinion is divided as to which gate provided access to it and what that road represents. Some observers maintain that it is the modern A1, which runs through Aldersgate from its start at St Paul's. Others believe that it ran through Bishopsgate along what is now the A10. Ermine Street is cited running through Cripplegate, linking Aldersgate Street for the north, to York (Eburacum) and then on to Hadrian's Wall. Edward Conybeare, writing in 1903, blamed much of this muddle on 'the conjectures of 17th-century antiquarianism' and especially Geoffrey of Monmouth for misleading 'many succeeding authorities'. Like those they built in Italy, there is no reason to suppose that the Romans gave names to roads in Britain. The use of the term 'street' adopted by the English is from the Latin *via strata* to describe something more than a mere track. Even supposedly authoritative maps offer a variety of Watling Streets and Ermine Streets branching in all directions across the land, some based on local tradition and others on learned judgements handed down and now used in the most casual way as fact. The London Stone, still extant in Cannon Street, was long thought to have been Londinium's *Milliarium Aureum* (Golden Milestone), a common reference point from which all distances were measured. Already an ancient and mysterious object in Shakespeare's day, William Blake and Charles Dickens helped perpetuate it as one of the capital's most mysterious relics since at least the Middle Ages and probably much earlier. By the nineteenth century the various roads from London were measured from ten or eleven different places, from Whitechapel church in the east, Hyde Park Corner in the west, and the south side of London Bridge. An old water tank known as 'The Standard' in Cornhill appears to have measured the roads north. One idea was to utilise the grand new centre of communications, the Post Office building in St Martin's Le Grand, appropriately fronted by an obelisk that would become a London imitation of that which stood in the Forum of ancient Rome, inscribed with the names and distances of large provincial towns. This was not adopted and so, at least by 1853, the Great North Road was started at St Paul's for Newgate Street and St Martin's Le Grand for Aldersgate. Aldersgate Street was designated by the Ministry of Transport in 1921 the A1 trunk route, the longest numbered road in the United Kingdom at 409 miles long connecting London with Edinburgh.

The line of London Wall after Aldersgate is preserved in the cellar of The Raglan pub. It would be possible to follow it above ground by taking the rear exit out of the pub into one of the meanest alleyways, even by City of London standards, past the north side of the church of St Anne and St Agnes and out through a gate into

Noble Street to meet up with the south-west corner of the Roman fort. Since this is not a public right of way, it's a matter of continuing south down Aldersgate and left into Gresham Street for the pretty little church of St Anne & St Agnes, first mentioned in 1467 as St Anne and St Agnes-within-Aldersgate. Rebuilt by Sir Christopher Wren after the Great Fire, it was badly damaged by bombing during the Second World War. The Lutheran Church assisted in its restoration according to Wren's design, and in 1966 dedicated it for Lutheran worship. Set within another small green public space, the church is flanked by part of the bombed shell of the church, a stark reminder of how much of the City of London looked sixty years ago when approximately 50 acres, or 14 per cent, of it was destroyed by enemy bombing. At the west end of the church, behind the steeple wall and gated off from public access, is the slender alleyway separating this house of worship with that of The Lord Raglan. The gate encloses a small grassed area beneath which runs the line of London Wall. Like all of these tiny green oases dotted about the City, it is immaculately kept. I don't think I've ever spent a day in the Square Mile without seeing a Corporation of London groundsman tending these incredibly important havens. Such a keeper was busily watering this patch when I was rooting around. I asked if I could step inside the gate to take a picture. 'No problem' he replied, without asking my reasons. It was not, after all, a regular tourist attraction or a scene of any significance, so he could have told me where to go. But I told him what I was up to and he appeared to be genuinely interested. Afterwards I took him the few yards down into Noble Street and pointed into the massive trench that comprises the west side of this road. I showed him the short length of Roman Wall foundation 15ft below running in the direction of the church, which is much thicker and more robust than the curve of ragstone representing the southwest corner of the Roman fort. Clearly visible along the route of the remains of the Wall is where the original wall was thickened when it was incorporated into the City Wall and probably heightened at the same time. 'What d'yer know?' the groundsman said through a smile as wide as the trench, 'all the time I been workin' here, I never knew none of that.' I thanked him for letting me take my picture and he thanked me for giving him something to tell his kids when he got home.

London's Roman fort lies on the edge of the upper Walbrook valley on the north-eastern shoulder of high ground centred on Ludgate Hill. This was a marginal area in the early development of Roman London, although it must have been attractive to early settlers. What evidence of population there is, however, suggests a date sometime after AD 70 as the Roman settlement expanded west, but it's hardly feasible that only the Romans saw the value of this prime location. Indeed, when the Museum of London was established in 1976 as part of the Barbican Estate, new areas of City landscape were examined throwing up evidence of Bronze Age occupation and prehistoric features dated to the late first century AD, prior to the early Roman occupation. But London, as a City, is a Roman invention, of that there is no doubt. Reconstruction of Londinium following the Boudican revolt of AD 61 was initially slow, taking as long as ten

21 Photograph of south-west corner of the Roman Fort and City Wall, Noble Street

years before many of the buildings were re-established. Things picked up after AD 70 perhaps as part of an ambitious public building programme. This was followed by a devastating fire in about AD 125 that destroyed a large area of the western part of the settlement. The subsequent reorganisation and rebuilding saw the area to the north-west, which was untouched by the fire, cleared of its few timber buildings. Construction of the fort was begun that same year together with the neighbouring amphitheatre where topsoil was removed and brickearth laid to level the fort area. Whereas the amphitheatre utilised a natural hollow of the Walbrook valley, the fort took advantage of the higher ground. Both were probably part of a concerted State enterprise in so far as the use of stone was an officially sourced building material.

Although wide open to speculation, the fort may have come about as an opportunity for the authorities looking to consolidate accommodation for soldiers serving in Londinium. Before the Romans established their permanent fortresses in Britain, they built large, defensive enclosures either to provide their legion and auxiliary groups with a long-term home, or as a summer campaign base or winter quarters. Known as vexillation fortresses and mainly found in the Midlands and southern Britain, they were built of timber and turf and protected by a ditch. The original Londinium garrison probably held the typical infantry cohort with barrack blocks, workshops, stores, a granary, the military headquarters building and commander's accommodation. Later, and with Rome no longer poised to continue expansion of the Empire, an important part of Londinium's

22 Photograph of culvert, south-west corner of the Roman fort and City Wall, Noble Street

consolidation would have been the strengthening of the fort with stone walls and towers to provide platforms for artillery. As a location for a defensive stronghold this higher ground offered a clear and unobstructed view, with the Walbrook creek to the east, the Fleet to the west and the swampy moors to the north as added defences.

Excavations by the Museum of London between 1992 and 2000 produced new evidence relating to the Roman fort first identified by the post-war pioneering archaeologist, Professor W.F. Grimes, who investigated bomb damaged sites in the years immediately following the Second World War. Norman Cook, the Keeper of the Guildhall Museum, observed the remains of the Wall as it appeared in the 1950s, poking through 'now and again from its later brick accretions', its line preserved by continued use of the same foundation laid by the Romans. Originally there were three individual trenches cut as part of the excavations carried out in Noble Street for the Roman & Medieval London Excavation Council. The one revealing the square foundation at the south-west corner of the fort represented a number of towers that provided access to the sentry walk around the fort and later the City Walls. The second trench midway along Noble Street showed not only the foundations of the masonry thickening added when the City Wall was built, but also the foundations of the fort wall itself. The excavation opposite the ruins of nos. 12 and 13 Noble Street revealed a cross-section of the ramp, or bank of clay, built on the inside of the City Wall. When freshly cut this section showed the bank built inside the later Wall. Beneath it and disturbed by its foundations was part of the earlier bank of the same reddish brick earth constructed inside the original fort wall. Also revealed was the layer of gravel, representing the road which ran at the foot of this bank round the whole of the fort's internal perimeter, and it was the presence of a coin dated to the 180s found in the Wall thickening that remains a prime source of dating evidence. After 1968 such archaeological excavations were undertaken by the Guildhall Museum, mostly in the form of salvage work during the frenetic redevelopment of bomb-damaged properties.

Professor Grimes speculated that it is unlikely that the advantageous terrain at this point was the sole reason for the choice of location for London's fort. There may have been a bipartite division of the City constituting a military centre west of the Walbrook and the civilian centre to the east. Supporting this view is the unusually large size of the fort. Professor Grimes first established the overall dimensions to be 760ft (232m) from north to south and 710ft (216m) from east to west, occupying an area of around 11.5 acres. In today's terms we can follow an exposed archaeological trail the entire length of the west wall and a large part of the north. The remains of the south wall disappear under Noble Street towards 25 Gresham Street and then in a line to Albermanbury, clipping the north-east corner of the Guildhall Library. The east wall then follows the course of Aldermanbury, under London Wall, to the north east of St Alphage Garden. Its size, equivalent to the largest contemporary forts, begs the question why was it built here, in a part of Britain generally considered to be peaceful and civilised, if not to define Londinium's strategic and economic importance. There is thought to have been only one other comparable military establishment in the whole of south-east England at this time, at Dover, which adds to the notion that the fort at Londinium must have had a very particular purpose.

Recent excavations have revealed much new information about the fort's internal layout, refuelling debate about its function and its garrison. It was long thought to have housed the 1000-strong bodyguard of the provincial governor, but it's now clear that it was capable of accommodating a much larger force. The fort pre-dates the City Wall by a century. Saxon attacks notwithstanding, the decision to build the Wall may also have its roots in the invasion of northern Britain by the Scots who overran Hadrian's Wall in the AD 180s. It may also have been as a result of the political crisis of the AD 190s when Septimus Severus and the governor of Britain, Claudius Albinus, both claimed the right to succession as Emperor. It was Severus that divided Roman Britain into two provinces: Britannia Superior with Londinium as its capital and Eboracum (York) as the capital of Brittannia Inferior, a legacy that survives to this day in the so-called North South Divide. Albinus may have had the Wall constructed to protect his interest, but that seems unlikely. Severus's conquest over the Scots is thought to have revived Londinium's fortunes in the early third century, although the more generally held view now is that London's fortunes declined in the last half of the second century. The fort may have fallen out of use soon after, but the military did not abandon Londinium completely. This later history of the fort remains obscure. The internal buildings do not seem to have remained in use much beyond the end of the second century AD, although some of the internal roads continued to be resurfaced for a time after the demolition of the barracks around the third and fourth centuries. It is thought that the whole area was abandoned between the fourth and eleventh centuries and developed in the first half of the twelfth with substantial high-status buildings built from recycled Roman building materials, some with cellars. In his interim report in 1968, Professor Grimes remarked that: 'Of the many problems relating to the fort that are likely to remain unsolved one of the chief is that of its later history... It is not therefore possible to say whether the fort continued a separate existence after it was incorporated into the City's defences... or whether its east and west walls were removed and its area made one with the civil settlement.'

Part of the fort/City Wall survives in places to a height of 8ft. For the most part it is medieval on Roman, the different building techniques apparent in the use of ragstone courses alternating with layers of tiles, facings and stonework, which in turn supports nineteenth-century construction. About midway along Noble Street these remains effectively become a unique garden terrace for one of the largest and finest of the City's Livery Halls, that belonging to the Worshipful Company of Plaisterers.

The polished façade acting as a contradictory backdrop to the ragged ruins frames a view of richly panelled walls and decorative sunken ceiling panels illuminated by rows of basket type chandeliers. Granted its charter by King Henry VII in 1501, the reflected grandeur of bygone eras sits remarkably easily as part of the ultra-sophisticated One London Wall, the latest (at the time of writing) and one of the most prestigious commercial developments dominating this corner of the City. Full planning permission involved the creation of a new office building comprising ground, basement and twelve upper floors to include the retention and alteration of the existing Plaisterer's Hall, the landscaping of adjacent open space and improvements to the setting of the Roman Wall, all subject to the rigorous scrutiny of the neighbours, the Museum of London. The selling agents describe One London Wall as being 'at one with its surroundings', while in

23 Photograph of Roman fort west wall and Plaisterers' Hall, Noble Street

reality it simultaneously complements as much as it eclipses. This 'unreservedly modern, towering fusion of glass and steel on a Portland stone base' is said to 'sit naturally on the 2000-year-old London Wall, effortlessly blending into its historic environment'. Moreover, 'the building's sleek curves follow the line of the original wall as it steps up from the lower level buildings on the west to meet the higher buildings on London Wall'.

London Wall is the name given to the City thoroughfare running from Bishopsgate to Aldersgate Street. Constructed in 1959, its route at the end of Noble Street passes over the site of the original West Gate of the Roman fort, and leaves stranded the largest lump of Roman Wall left standing under the oceanic sweep of One London Wall.

None of the London perambulators before the 1960s make mention of the fort's West Gate in their accounts of the City Wall, its discovery awaiting the building of the new thoroughfare. Prior to this great remodelling of the City there were only the trenches dug by Grimes and occasional glimpses of medieval masonry surrounded by modern brick along the line of the Wall. They also offered the only evidence of the dramatic change in ground level that had taken place over the past 1900 years. Today we can peer down 15ft or more of history, back to the level of the Roman city, whereas before the bombs dropped and the new London emerged, the present street level was maintained without a break with Noble Street leading into Falcon Square, Silver Street and City Wells Street, 'just Lanes in a devastated and uninhabited area', lamented Cook. Another small stretch of

24 Photograph of Roman fort west wall by London Wall

ancient City Wall was visible either side of Windsor Court, which occupied the area immediately north of the new road. Peering over the concrete parapet of today's Barbican Highwalk is to look down onto the level of Roman London and a surviving bastion, perhaps one of the two aspects of London's Wall with which Londoners and visitors alike are most familiar, the other being the great chunk of Wall on Tower Hill.

There are no signs or indicators of any sort to lure the visitor down to the Roman level. In the summer the carefully manicured lawns can be littered with City workers enjoying lunch, otherwise it appears distinctly off-limits. The discreet slip road leads down to 140 London Wall and the underground car park, but it is not a pedestrian walkway. Directly ahead at the bottom is 140 London Wall's lower reception area. Outside, smokers huddle under the Highwalk viewing interlopers with suspicion, or possibly feeling a little bit silly. There is the distinct feeling about this place that it is private. On my first visit I felt sure that a security guard would appear until I realised that there is a public footpath hugging the side of the building. Even though the grass screams out the immortal warning, you are not obliged to keep off. In fact there is a point of entry at the mouth of the bastion, inviting exploration.

Standing on this same spot in the 1950s, only the top half of the bastion stood above ground, with its greater proportion in the form of a cellar awaiting excavation. Even so, the external masonry clearly demonstrated mostly medieval construction together with much in the way of later brickwork patching.

The remains of the medieval arrow slit was then visible at street level with the traces of the other slit above it made into a window. Of the Roman fort West Gate, there was no visible trace. Today, the remains are preserved in a concrete bunker under the road and can be seen by arrangement with the Museum of London. Although regular half-hour tours take place on selected days during the week and occasionally on a Sunday, I was fortunate to be met by Jackie Kielty, one of the Museum curators and author of the report on small finds at Roman and Medieval Cripplegate, who kindly offered to show me around.

The entrance to the chamber is between the underground car park and 140 London Wall. On entry Jackie explained that these remains were rescued when the top priority was the rejuvenation of a war-torn City. The thrusting new thoroughfare was one of a number embracing the motor car, which generated the underground car park that created the space for the preservation of this unique piece of London archaeology. The topographical difficulties in combining the ancient with the ultra-new are challenging enough today, so a measure of credit is due to the often criticised post-war planners. While conditions in the resulting vault fail to match those found at the Guildhall Amphitheatre, or under Merrill Lynch, there is something appealing and rare about entering what might pass for a tomb. It's as private as it is raw, almost as though it has just been constructed and awaiting the more sanitised setting we have become used to.

A yellowing sign declares the remains to consist of the north guard room, one gravelled roadway and the central piers of the gate, which when complete had a second roadway and guard room to the south. The gate stood at the west end of the main street through the fort, which was built in the late first century AD. Below the sign sits a model, itself of some considerable age, offering a romantic idea of how the large blocks of sandstone and rubble walls connected. Some of these blocks, which form the base, weigh over half a ton with the Lewis holes clearly visible. These are holes in cut stones for lifting and supporting by means of the particular Lewis lifting device, or hook, to be used. The remaining masonry consists mostly of Kentish ragstone, except for some footings of dressed stone, two of which comprise the entrance to the guardroom house. The gouge marks cut into the surface of these were caused by the drag of lower bolts from an iron gate, a small detail but one of those that bring such exhibits to life. The guard room opening onto the gravel road is divided in two by stone piers that would have supported arches spanning the gates. Each passage was wide enough for a cart and each had a pair of heavy wooden doors. Either in the fourth century or the medieval period, or whenever it was that Aldersgate superseded this gate, the passageway was blocked with massive stones. These were removed in the 1960s to reveal at the base of the footings the lower hinge recesses that once bore the considerable weight of the hefty wooden gates. The comparatively modest width of the original fort wall can also be determined with no attempt made to bind or joint the internal thickening added when it was incorporated into the City Wall.

25 Photograph of Roman fort West Gate, London Wall

As part of the West Gate tour, the neighbouring bastion is explained within the context of the City Wall, although the difficulties in trying to negotiate such a complex piece of physical history are all too apparent on closer inspection.

Many visitors automatically assume that the tower is Roman, built as part of the Wall, whereas it is a combination of building techniques across all eras. In 1257 Henry III 'caused the walles of this Citie, which was sore decaied and destitute of towers, to be repaired in more seemely wise than before.' In 1900, before it was fully excavated, William Lethaby expressed no doubt that the medieval arrangement closely followed the Roman scheme. The openings in the original bastions would, he supposed, have been wider with a semicircular brick arch over them. 60 to 70yds apart, about 20ft round at the front and projecting out about 16ft, they would have stood about 15–16ft higher than the parapet walk on the main Wall rising in a slope from the ground with possibly two stories, each containing three large openings. The medieval window and arrowslit that before 1960 could be seen at street level now forms the first level of the tower. Its face also includes socket holes used to support the wooden scaffolding when it was built, and at the top are the remains of a band of decorative knapped flints. Where the medieval meets the Roman is in the lower interior, again largely unseen by investigators when it was a cellar. Here Roman bricks, or reused roofing tiles are exposed on the line of the original fort wall that were antique when the thickening was added.

26 Photograph of West Wall Monkwell Street bastion, south side

27 Photograph of West Wall Monkwell Street bastion, north side

28 Photograph of West Wall Barber-Surgeons' Hall bastion

During the later medieval period these towers were let as simple dwellings. A plan of this one in the eighteenth century shows the property transferred to a Mr Christopher Morrison. The semicircular dwelling had a near-30ft frontage facing onto a yard measuring 14.5ft×30ft facing Mugwell Street, later Monkwell Street, now partly Monkwell Square. Complete with a brick shed built over the site of the Roman fort West Gate, tiny Windsor Court led out from the yard into Mugwell Street. Later additions are the remains of a brick stairway and fireplace, and the whole of the interior was refaced with nineteenth-century brick in the change from residential to industrial use when much of the medieval stone wall was demolished. Before the 1960s, that piece extending north consisted of rubble masonry with frequent and irregular tile bonding courses containing re-used Roman material. Even then it stood at a considerable height. Only after the bombing in 1940 did it reveal its true dimensions, complete with an arch attaching the lower half of the bastion. Norman Cook describes next a semicircular hole in the ground which, he maintains, before the bombing was incorporated into a warehouse which had a rounded end. This semicircular foundation was, in fact, used in the creation of an apsidal end for the Barber-Surgeons' Hall, itself destroyed by enemy bombs in 1940.

Today a garden separates the old from the new as one of only ten Livery company gardens remaining in the City. There has been a garden on this spot since medieval times when the inner walk areas of the City Wall began to be utilised by private property owners. The present garden was begun in 1987 on what was then

29 Photograph of West Wall Barber Surgeon's Hall bastion interior

still a derelict bomb site. Influenced by herbalist John Gerrard, who was Master of the Surgeons' Company in 1607, the garden boasts a formal planting and a larger informal area, and forty-five small plots divided into four areas corresponding to different uses of herbs and medicinal plants. The Barber-Surgeons' Company moved from their Livery Hall near the Tower of London to this location in 1607 when it incorporated the remains of the medieval tower as the base of its new courtroom. Immediately north of this apse more buildings were added in the 1630s, including an anatomy theatre designed by Inigo Jones. The Hall was badly damaged in the Great Fire and was rebuilt. These buildings were in turn partly demolished in 1863–4 and then completely destroyed by German bombing in 1940. The Hall we see today took thirty years to replace in seeking an agreement with the Corporation of London to preserve what remained of London's Wall and for it to be free from obstruction. It was eventually agreed to rebuild back from the Wall, while echoing the apse in the new Great Hall.

Part of the Wall is also preserved and reflects the many alterations over time from the twelfth to the nineteenth centuries in its stone and brickwork patching. This leads to the third and final bastion that represents the north-west corner of the Roman fort, which in turn accounts for the angular kink in an otherwise gentle arc when it was incorporated into the City Wall. Excavations carried out at the turn of the twentieth century showed that the base of this tower was buried by 18ft of accumulated soil, giving it a total height of approximately 31ft. The bottom 4ft were deemed to be of Roman workmanship with all else above

30 Nineteenth-century illustration of Cripplegate Bastion, St Giles' Churchyard

that level medieval and later. The same as the other bastions along this stretch of
the City Wall, this one was found to be hollow. During the clearance of bomb
damage still underway in the 1950s, it was possible to see for the first time in
centuries the base of the tower, its diameter measuring about 37ft. 6ft above the
ground level, the ragstone and mortar construction gave way to a mixture of the
same, as well as dressed stone before a slight shoulder two thirds of the way up
supporting regular courses of stone blocks. The medieval masonry continued for
several more courses, although the top had been levelled off and rebuilt over more
recent years. Today this solid protuberance squats partially in the water feature
created during the Barbican Estate development built to echo the defensive ditch
around the Wall. Rising to almost two thirds its original height, the tower over
time became half buried in earth dumped to raise the level of the churchyard of

31 Twenty-first-century photograph of Cripplegate Bastion, St Giles' Churchyard

St Giles' Cripplegate and was only fully uncovered during the creation of this centre of post-war optimism built in the new emerging architectural style.

There is something satisfying in the alliance of brutalism in this surviving symbol of medieval power. The stout metal gate strung across the footpath continues to do what a barbican is designed to and keeps people out. There are no signs that this is a private right of way, but it is. On one of my initial research trips I found the gate unlocked, but having subsequently checked with the Barbican Estate Office, I can confirm that this is part of the Barbican Residential Estate and is a private route for residents only. No public right of way exists and

32 Photograph of Cripplegate bastion interior

normally this gate would be closed and locked. Peeking through it, however, it
is possible to see that unlike the bastion at the far end, this one is not lined with
nineteenth-century brick and that the holes for the original floor joists can still
be seen.

In 1803 that part of it protruding above ground was considered to be the 'most
perfect' remaining fragment of the old City Defences. Several prints and engravings
from the time show the 'venerable remains' more than half buried, complete with
a substantial piece of battlemented Wall running off it. A thatched 'porch' nestled
between the two, presumably an entrance into the structure. To appreciate just
how much the ground level was raised since Roman times, the apartment blocks
flanking these remains would be missing their lower floor completely. Another
bastion base follows the line of the water feature to another surviving section of
City Wall, formerly the Roman fort north wall. To appreciate them better requires
backtracking to the point of entry on the higher, modern ground where there are
steps up to the Museum of London and other destinations and steps down back
to the Roman level. Passing by the front of Barber-Surgeons' Hall in Monkwell
Square and out into Wood Street, at the north end of the latter is the entrance to
St Giles' Terrace and the soothing sound of water playing on another severe lake
at the heart of the Barbican Estate. Opened in 1969, this dramatic statement was
designed for City professionals with the underlying intention of creating a small
walled town to provide privacy and the opportunity to move freely around in a
constantly changing perspective of hard and soft landscape features. With over

2000 flats, the various levels create a total pedestrian area almost twice the actual size of the site.

One of the few remaining medieval churches in the City of London, St Giles' Cripplegate sits like a stranded stone whale on a beach of hard fired mud. Nothing is known about the early Saxon church, other than it was probably no more than a small chantry, or chapel, made of wattle and daub. The Norman church that stood here was sometime during the Middle Ages dedicated to St Giles, the patron saint of beggars and cripples. As the population of the parish increased so the church was enlarged and in 1394 was rebuilt in the perpendicular style. Accounts have it that during the Great Plague of 1665 an estimated 5–8000 parishioners of St Giles' Cripplegate succumbed to the disease. This is said to have led to the graveyard being extended to the City Wall in order to accommodate the dead. Some were buried in the church itself and others in plague pits close by, but the majority were interred in the wake of London Wall, raising the level of the ground by several feet. The church suffered serious damage by fire on three occasions and the plans for its restoration, drawn up in 1545, were only used after the Second World War when it suffered a direct hit on the north door and was showered with so many incendiary bombs that even the cement caught alight. Around the windows on the north wall the inside stonework has been left blackened to show the effect of this inferno. All that remained was the shell, the arcade in the chancel, the outside walls and the tower. On the right of the east window, part the medieval sedilia, where the priests sat, and the piscina, where they disposed of the excess communion wine, has been left exposed. The tiles in the arch are of Roman origin and in Queen Victoria's reign the outside walls were surfaced with ragstone brought from Kent, the same as that used by the Romans to build the City Wall.

Walter G. Bell wrote of this spot in 1937: 'With its well-kept lawns and beds of summer flowers, it is the most delightful nature spot in the City'. Today only a significant number of weeds force their way through the thoroughly tiled surface. The Great Cripplegate bastion opposite was before the war 'small and insignificant, rising to a height of only a few feet', although Bell knew through previous examinations that its lowest courses showed clear evidence of Roman workmanship. The bastion, then in its churchyard setting, stood at an outward angle of the City Wall, much fuller than the usual half-circle. The line of the Wall heading southward could be traced in the buildings of the time, offering 'a curious appearance filling all of the land once occupied by a projecting bastion'. The tower, now reflected in the water, is a reminder of the days when this 'great store of verie good fish, of diverse sorts' was reduced to a narrow, filthy channel, often blocked altogether with waste. In this, the church of St Giles' Cripplegate was largely to blame. Founded in 1090 it immediately attracted the growth of a suburb outside the City Wall, which in turn took its toll on the amenity. In 1354 the ditch overflowed to such an extent that it forced a huge wave of detritus over the banks of the Tower of London. One Anthony Munday, continuing Stow's account of Cripplegate parish, talks of a

33 Photograph of Roman fort north wall bastion foundation

route through part of the churchyard crossing what was known as the 'Tower Ditch'. In 1379, John Philpot, Mayor of London, charged every household 5*d* or a day's pay towards its upkeep. The Ten Year Toll placed by Richard II also included ditch maintenance to that of repairs to the Wall. Nearly a century later and Ralph Josceline, the mayor of London, 'caused the whole Ditch to be cast and cleansed'. But over time with the absence of imposed charges for its cleaning and with profits to be made letting out the banks, it fell into decay. What might be described as a 'last-ditch' effort was made in 1595 when it was cleaned out and widened, only for it to quickly fill up again due to the raising of the adjoining land. Eventually the Wall itself became enclosed in buildings, degrading any notion of a practical defence system, more a property boundary, and so the ditch became redundant.

It was not until the landscaping of the late 1960s and early 1970s for the Barbican development that the foundation of another bastion was recovered along this north wall which, like its more substantial neighbour, also dips its toe into the water feature.

This is very probably the tower that formed part of the famous thirteenth-century hermitage of St James-in-the-Wall situated opposite St Giles' church. The City records until the Reformation abound with references to hermits living along London Wall. Although the terms anker or anchorite and hermit are often used interchangeably, there was difference between the two. A hermit generally lived a cosmetically solitary life but was free to wander about and to socialise, whereas an anker or anchorite was sealed in a cell which he or she never left, often ending their career being buried beneath the floor of the cell. These recluses were visited by devout people who regarded their sacrifice in excluding themselves from the world in a life of prayer as a form of sanctity. To become an anker or anchorite meant living almost a half death, even having part of the funeral service read over them on adopting the role. Their only means of support was the charity taken from the devout. Anything above and beyond their own personal requirements was given as relief to Christ's poor. The Cripplegate hermitage may have been founded by the Crown shortly after the Norman Conquest, as it owed much to royal grants and protection. It was certainly in existence in the reign of King John, who ordered an enquiry about a house which had belonged to Warin the hermit of Cripplegate. Although Brother Warin was appointed by King Richard I, he had been chaplain to King John's son Henry (afterwards Henry III) and John seems to have had a special regard for him. The resident recluse in 1311 was Thomas de Wreford who went somewhat beyond his remit in hearing confessions, administering sacrament and offering indulgences.

At various times during its vacancy the Cripplegate cell was given over by the Sovereign to the Mayor of London and to the Constable of the Tower. Edward I on several occasions appointed wardens to protect the goods and fabric of the chapel on the death of the hermit. This, however, proved unsatisfactory and so in 1341 the king made over his rights to the abbot of Garendon. A chantry chapel was endowed by the Countess of Pembroke so that Masses might be said for the soul of Aymer de Valence, the 2nd Earl of Pembroke, a Franco-English nobleman with strong connections to both Royal houses. As well as the cell at Bishopsgate, the hermitage of Cripplegate appears to have been an earlier and more important foundation. Come the Dissolution, however, and it was destroyed along with all the rest. In its last stage the Cripplegate cell was the property of the Clothworkers' Company and had become Lambe's Chapel attaching Lambe's Almshouses, which stood at the upper end of Monkwell Street. The builder was a wealthy cloth merchant who, as a gentleman of Henry VIII's

34 Photograph of Roman fort north wall remains

chapel, benefited from the dissolution. Beneath the chapel was the crypt of the ancient hermitage of St James-in-the Wall, which was removed to Mark Lane in 1872 where it survives to this day. The *Illustrated London News* for April 1859 has a print of Lambe's Chapel in Monkwell Street, with the remains of the old City Wall bastion beside it.

In 1803 the particularly 'fine battlemented section of the Wall' opposite St Giles' church had become 'tufted with wild plants' and was deemed to be a danger. Another reason for its removal given in the same year was 'by reason of the frequent nuisances committed by some of the louest class of people, who had been suffered to inhabit the adjoining premises'. What remains of it can be seen as a reasonable stretch from across the water standing on Roman foundations about two thirds of its original height.

Its interior face has been robbed of its facing stones, with only the core exposed. In the 1950s it was covered in places with the remains of a pebbly concrete, all that was left of the modern buildings that had been erected against it. A Standing Structure Recording was taken of it and the neighbouring bastions by the Museum of London in December 1992. As well as the known Roman, medieval and post-medieval features, parts of the Roman fabric were then newly interpreted as belonging to the original north wall of the fort. There were possible modifications to the outer face, perhaps when it was incorporated in the defensive wall around the city, but curiously with no thickening on the inner face of the fort wall.

Returning to Wood Street, the aptly named Roman House nestles on the corner with Fore Street. Carved into its Portland stone wall, is a memorial to Adolph Hitler's failure in achieving his initial plan for the invasion of Britain. From September 1940 to the spring of 1941 German bombers flew regular raids on British cities in what became known as the Blitz, a tactic employed to break the morale of the British people and make it impossible for the government to continue the war. London was bombed almost continuously from 7 September to 12 November 1940 and an estimated 13,000 people were killed. Although the capital continued to be attacked, other major cities became targets. The dedication reads: 'On this site at 12.25am on the 25th August 1940 fell the first bomb on the City of London in the Second World War.' On the other side of the same building towards St Alphage Garden are two other commemorations to the successful occupation of these shores almost two thousand years previously. A blue plaque and Museum of London panel mark the site of the original northern entrance to the Roman fort that eventually gave way to Cripplegate, a word derived from the Anglo-Saxon 'cruplegate', meaning a covered way or tunnel running from the City Gate to the fortified watchtowers, or barbicans, along the City Wall. A thousand years later and such a covered way runs through the apartment block opposite, fortified by a metal gate preventing non-residents walking the line of the Wall.

Another interpretation of the name Cripplegate is that cripples begged here, believing that entry into the City at this gate cured the lame. With the church close by dedicated to St Giles, the patron saint of cripples, this has some justification. The gate is mentioned in tenth- and eleventh-century documents, for example in the *History of Edmund, King of the East Angles*, written in the year 1010, which records the body of the Martyr brought to London, 'in at Creplegate'. John Strype refers to the Charter of William the Conqueror, confirming the foundation of St Martin the Great College in London, granting all the land 'without the Postern, which is called Creplegate'. In the year 1090, Alfune is credited with the building of St Giles' church 'near the City Gate called in Latin *Porta contractorum*, or in the English tongue, Crepallsgate'. The substantial suburb born of St Giles was by no means the most salubrious in or around London. By the sixteenth century it had become the natural haunt of 'thieves, vagabonds and actors'. William Shakespeare lived at the corner of Monkwell Street and Silver Street, and Grub Street is perhaps the most famous of all the Barbican streets, described by Samuel Johnson as 'much inhabited by writers of small histories, dictionaries and temporary poems'.

Despite the area's unsavoury reputation, or perhaps because of it, the Brewers of London whose Hall was nearby, rebuilt the gate in 1244 and again in 1491 at a cost of 400*m*. And it was outside Cripplegate that the less noble members of Sir Thomas Wyatt's rebellion were executed. On the death of Edward VI in July 1553, the Duke of Northumberland attempted to put his daughter-in-law, Lady Jane Grey, upon the throne, but it came to nothing with Mary, eldest daughter of Henry VIII, crowned queen that same month. A devout Catholic,

35 Nineteenth-century illustration of the last remains of Cripplegate Postern

Mary decided on a marriage best capable of fostering the faith in her realm. When her marriage to Philip of Spain was announced, Sir Thomas Wyatt feared for the fate of England and evolved a plot to raise armies in different parts of the country to converge on London. Like many a plotter in Tudor times Wyatt was betrayed, but he went ahead regardless, marching on the capital at the head of 3000 men. After a minor skirmish, however, the morale of his men evaporated rapidly and the promised popular support was nowhere to be found. Wyatt reached Ludgate on the morning of 8 February 1554, but found it barred against him. He retreated as far as Temple Bar, where he surrendered. He was then taken to the Tower of London where he was tried for treason, found guilty, and executed. Four bloody years later and the Protestant Queen Elizabeth made a State entry into the City of London by Cripplegate, passing the spot in her State Carriage where Wyatt's anti-Catholic supporters had been executed. Cripplegate thereafter enjoyed mostly a peaceful history, apart from a second association with men of plot and intrigue.

The Fifth Monarchy, or Fifth Kingdom, refers to an interpretation of prophecies in the biblical books of Daniel and Revelation. Four kingdoms or eras in history: the Babylonian, Persian, Greek and Roman Empires would be followed by the Fifth Kingdom, ruled by a son of man (interpreted as the Papacy) who would reign for 1000 years, ending at the Millennium when Christ would physically reign on Earth. The Fifth Monarchists regarded the English Civil War and the beheading of King Charles I in 1649 as a necessary prelude to the movement. When Oliver Cromwell dissolved the Purged Parliament in April 1653, the Fifth Monarchists hailed him as a second Moses, leading God's chosen people to the Promised Land. The sudden dissolution of the Nominated Assembly and the establishment of Cromwell's Protectorate in December 1653, however, was taken as a betrayal and the key Monarchy Men were imprisoned after denouncing Cromwell. The sect continued to agitate against the Protectorate until 1657 when another plot was discovered. After the restoration of Charles II in 1660, all the City Gates were unhinged and the portcullises wedged open making them useless for defence. This prompted a desperate Fifth Monarchy uprising in January 1661, which put the whole of the City into a state of alarm. The agitators rampaged through the City, charging the Watch on duty at Bishopsgate before doubling back to Cripplegate. Hearing that a troop of horse was coming, they retreated to Hampstead for the night. Some were captured next morning, and the rest dispersed. Others rallied and returned to the City through Cripplegate, fighting a fierce battle with the Trained Bands in Wood Street where two of them were killed and their leader, Venner, was wounded. Colonel Cox, another leader, posted ten men in a neighbouring alehouse, which was held until seven of the dissenters had been killed. Having by now lost twenty men, they fled. Of the fourteen captured, eleven were tried and executed. Twenty of the king's men and about the same number of Trained Band citizens and others had been killed. The failure of the rising was followed by repressive legislation aimed at the suppression of all nonconformist sects. After 1661 Cripplegate was variously leased as accommodation or used as a gaol for low-level offenders such as debtors and trespassers. After being damaged in the Great Fire five years later it was 'Repaired and Beautified' with the rooms over the Gate set aside for the City Water Bailiff. Cripplegate survived another century as a ceremonial entrance before its demolition in 1760.

Nothing survives of pre-1940s London in this immediate quarter, only bits of its most ancient fabric careering through the concrete, glass and steel like an inconvenient elderly relative. The church dedicated to St Alphage was established east of today's Wood Street in the eleventh century, utilising the inner face of City Wall as its northern boundary. During the civil wars fought in medieval England from 1455 to 1487 between the Houses of Lancaster and York, Ralph Josceline, the Lord Mayor of London, encouraged the Great Twelve Livery companies of the City of London to set about repairing part of the Wall between Aldgate and Aldersgate. For this they used clay dug from the Moor Fields outside the City Wall to make bricks and chalk from Kent to be burnt into Lime. The Skinners' Company completed that part of the Wall between Aldgate and Bevis Marks towards Bishopsgate, the Mayor and his Drapers' Company built the section between Bishopsgate and All Hallows church towards Moorgate, with the greater part repaired by the executors of Sir John Crosby, a late Alderman. Other companies repaired the rest, including this stretch, as far as Cripplegate. From there the Goldsmiths repaired the Wall as far as Aldersgate. The best evidence of this major repair and restoration is the red and black decorative brickwork battlements seen from what is today St Alphage Garden, once the churchyard. St Alphage was rebuilt in 1532 and survived the Great Fire, but was rebuilt again in the eighteenth century.

In 1872 the churchyard had become the small public garden we see today. A slowly disintegrating slab of limestone bolted underneath the decorative fifteenth-century brickwork contains the solemn declaration delivered by George Kemp M.A. Rector, and churchwardens William Smith and G.R. Tattersall, that the garden was brought about by an Act of Parliament in 1872. The church was rebuilt again in 1919, after the first air raid on the City, but was pulled down in 1923 leaving just the tower standing and the impressive section of London Wall, the longest span in public view until the 1960s. This pleasant open space includes flowerbeds, trees and seating, as well as a gate leading into Salters' Garden, which was reopened in 1995 to commemorate the 600th anniversary of the Worshipful Company of Salters. Open to the public on weekdays, this external face of the Wall is sunk below the modern road level. Whereas today it's a simple matter of passing into the garden through a gate from St Alphage churchyard, attempting to do so after the war involved what Norman Cook described as 'a little clambering' over the bombed out ruins of more recent structures. If the garden is closed, the main entrance to Salters' Hall in Fore Street provides an excellent view of the damage this length of Wall has suffered over the centuries. Cellars that were cut into it have left a core just 18in thick at the western end. The inner side also indicates the amount of rebuilding and repair over time. But despite these ravages

36 Photograph of London Wall in St Alphage churchyard

there is much evidence remaining of the Wall's construction in the distinct types of rubble, stone and brick facing, and with knapped flints and pieces of tile used as decorative bands in the stonework.

Despite the improved access to either side face of the Wall, there is no exit point at the end of Salter's Garden to continue walking the line, only a set of steps leading up to the depressed windswept wasteland of Alphage Highwalk. Returning therefore to the gate in St Alphage and continuing east is to pass another ancient relic languishing in a kind of protective pit parallel with the London Wall thoroughfare. A notice put up by the Corporation of London tells us:

> These are the ruins of the fourteenth-century tower of the chapel of the Priory of Elsing Spital which was incorporated into the second church of St Alphage at the time of the Reformation. The original eleventh-century church which was dedicated to St Alphage, Archbishop of Canterbury who was killed by the Danes in 1012, lay further to the north against London Wall. Its ruins were demolished when the Priory chapel was taken over by the parish church. These remains were exposed when the surrounding buildings were destroyed by enemy action in 1940.

Beside this rather sad remnant is a grim underpass running beneath St Alphage Highwalk. Remains of the Roman Wall foundations doubtless lie beneath the tarmac but there is no indication of this passing into Fore Street.

37 Photograph of Salters' Garden

38 Photograph of St Alphage tower, London Wall

John Strype in 1720 describes Fore Street as being 'pretty broad and well inhabited' and 'lined with good, substantial houses'. Conversely, John Noorthouck in his *New History of London* written in 1773 recalls the same street as 'a narrow dirty lane of irregular and mean buildings'. In the reign of Henry III (1216–1272) when London really began to reek, the king had the first water pipes and public conveniences installed under the streets of the capital since Roman times. But these latrines could be dangerous places. In 1290 one John de Alyndon was mugged and murdered in one that stood somewhere along this stretch of London Wall. In 1312 'a certain man of Cheap Ward', while coming by night from a 'common privy in London Wall' had an argument with another man. The two quarrelled and fought and one of them was killed. Although Henry III was in effect London's first great sanitary engineer, the cost infuriated the ratepayers and so the capital put up with its own stench for the next five centuries. Also hereabouts was Lorimers' Hall, another Livery Hall, described by John Strype as 'a pretty, neat building adjoining London Wall'. There were also two posterns, or pedestrian gates, before Moorgate, one facing Basinghall Street and the other at the top of Aldermanbury, representing the north east corner of the Roman fort. Strype expands that it was in 1655 that the Wall was breached 'overagainst the North End of Aldermanbury; and another Postern made with double Gates for a Passage into Forestreet. And soon after, another near the North End of Bassinshawstreet, leading into the aforesaid Forestreet, formerly called the Postern leading into More-fields'. Victorian antiquarian

Walter Thornbury records workmen digging foundations for houses on the north-east side of the Aldermanbury Postern in 1857 and coming across a portion of the Roman wall strengthened by blind arches. Unfortunately the configuration of the 1960s London Wall thoroughfare and its Highwalks do not provide an easy diversion off Fore Street for the sites of these attractions, but there is nothing to see in any case, no sign or any clue as to what has gone before. The next clue to the route of the City Wall is at the junction of London Wall and another major thoroughfare named after the only City Gate to take its name from the landscape.

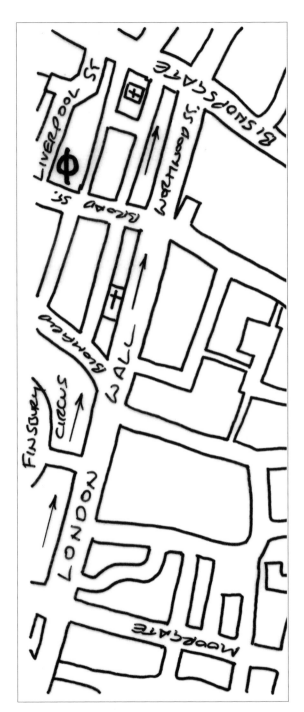

39 Map from Moorgate to Bishopsgate

5

Moorgate to Bishopsgate

The name Moorgate is derived from the wide expanse of swampy marsh anciently known as Moor Fields, or La More, which extended from Cripplegate to Bishopsgate. This 'mora' is mentioned in a Charter of William I, and William Fitzstephen describes it in 1170 as 'the great fen, which waters the walls of the city on the north'. It's thought there was no gate here in Roman times but that it was a later addition. Excavations have shown that the construction of the City Wall probably exacerbated the issue of poor drainage. Indeed, even by the early fourteenth century there was still sufficient water draining into the ditches to float a boat with six passengers. Stow refers to an 'iron grate on the channell which runneth into the watercourse of Walbrooke before ye come to the posterne called Moorgate'. The Walbrook is the small river or stream that once bisected the City. Today it runs underground from its source out of what were Moorfields towards the Bank of England and about 150ft west of the street named after the stream. Its presence is still felt by a discernible dip along Cannon Street where it runs about 30ft below ground as the London Bridge Sewer, disgorging its contents into the Thames from an outlet about 120ft west of Cannon Street Station. Where the eventual City Gate stood is marked by a blue plaque hidden behind a concrete leg holding up part of the London Metropolitan University on the north east corner of Moorgate and London Wall.

The first reference we have for a gate at this point is in 1415 when Thomas Falconer, the Lord Mayor of London, 'caused the Wall of the City to be broken towards Moorfields, and built the postern called Moorgate'. It came complete with 'a gate to be shut at night and at other fitting times' and was built for the ease of the citizens to walk 'upon causeways towards Islington and Hoxton'. Unfortunately, it failed to impress the residents of those hamlets. Hoxton inhabitants responded by enclosing the fields and harassing walkers from the City, and stopping archers practising on Hoxton Fields. Stow records the postern being rebuilt in 1472 and improved again in 1511 when Mayor Roger Achely 'caused Dikes and Bridges to be made, and the Ground to be levelled, and made more commodious for Passage'. During the next century the City Commissioners, among whose number ranked Inigo Jones as the Surveyor-General, were ordered to make a sewer to drain Moor-Ditch, a work already begun in 1633. Perhaps in celebration of this event, King Charles I made a State Entry into the City through Moorgate in 1641, the coolness of his reception, however, clear evidence of the City's view on the quarrel between King and Parliament. The following year, when he set up his Standard at Nottingham, the City's six regiments of militia were drilled and exercised in readiness on Moor Fields. Officers of Parliament were detailed to inspect and repair all the City Gates, posterns, portcullises, chains and posts, followed by the building of the largest fortification of London since the Romans built the Wall. This outer defence consisted of an immense trench with a circuit of 18 miles from Wapping to Westminster and with a corresponding trench south of the river. At intervals were twenty-four forts armed with 211 cannon. All ranks and ages of citizens took part in the construction, more than 20,000 working daily without pay from October 1642 to its completion the following May. But it was never put to the test. Within a few years the forts were dismantled, although traces of the great earthworks survived for a century and more.

By the time John Strype published his *Survey of London* (1720) the City Ditch had finally disappeared, its area entirely covered by houses, yards and gardens. The land had been raised so much that the dykes and bridges on Moor Fields were all covered, and yet it seemed to him that even 'if it be made Level with the Battlements of the City Wall, yet will it be little the dryer, such is the Moorish Nature of that Ground'. This is an interesting observation, as huge improvements had been made since 1606 when the ground outside the City Wall had been drained and raised to such a level that parts of it were already laid out with 'pleasant Walks, set with Trees for Shade and Ornament.' Brick Walls were built and their foundations secured with 'Vaults under Ground for Conveyance of the Water.' It was only a year earlier, in 1605, that Mayor Sir Leonard Halliday began all the 'Alteration, Time, Pains and Expence' required to transform this once 'unhealthful Place', not to mention the work carried out by the City Commissioners started twenty years later. Odd therefore that Strype fails to observe these improvements, more so when he recalls in 1672 (then aged twenty-nine) Moorgate, then 'being very old'. It was pulled down and a new one of stone erected to serve a 'great thoroughfare', so busy a route in fact that a separate postern was provided either side of the arch for foot passengers. Even a Hay Market was proposed on the former marsh, which hardly promotes the 'Moorish Nature' of the place. Daniel Defoe, writing just a few years after Strype published his *Survey*, describes 'a very beautiful gateway, the arch being near twenty foot high, which was done to give room for the city Train'd Bands to go through to the Artillery Ground, where they muster, and that they might march with their pikes advanc'd, for then they had pikemen in every regiment, as well in the army as in the militia'. This, he found, made the gate look a little out of shape, especially if the reason for its high arch was not known. Another reason for the height of the arch may have been to provide for the passage of hay wagons destined for the proposed Hay Market, but such conjecture was short lived as a little over thirty years after it was built, Moorgate joined the City Gates as surplus to requirements. Its materials were sold for £166 but later repurchased by the Corporation of London to be used to support the buttresses of the newly widened London Bridge centre arch.

The City Wall east of Moorgate was incorporated into the Bethlem Hospital, or Bedlam, as the asylum founded for lunatics became more commonly known. Formerly a priory acquired by the City Corporation in 1547 and re-established as the old Bishopsgate asylum, the magnificent baroque building designed by Robert Hooke was opened in 1676. On each of the two main floors huge galleries ran the length of the building, with open work iron grilles across the centre to divide the male and female wings. The only public institution for the treatment of mental disorders at the time, Bedlam became a popular tourist attraction where people flocked to see the patients chained in cells. In 1770 compassion was shown by the authorities when it was decided that 'the tranquillity of the patients' was being disturbed, so admission was restricted to ticket holders only. Perhaps its most enduring feature is the pair of bald-headed and half-naked figures that decorated the entrance gates. Created by the sculptor Caius Cibber, depicting 'Raving and Melancholy madness', the former looks defeated and vacant, while the latter is chained to a plinth, his face etched with pain and anguish. Despite its outward splendour, the building was reported to be insecure as early as 1800, one wing having been demolished the previous year. Built without foundations on the former marsh, its construction had been rushed and the materials used poor. With that and the inevitable overcrowding, the hospital moved to its third site at St George's Fields, Southwark in 1815, which survives today as part of the Imperial War Museum. The carved representations of Madness, doubtless embracing the mood of the City Fathers at the time, are now kept at the Royal Bethlem Hospital Museum in Kent, where the institution moved to in the 1930s. An issue of the *Gentleman's Magazine* in 1753 has an illustration of an inscribed stone found in the City Wall to the rear of Bethlem hospital, in the apartment of the apothecary, Mr. Weaver. Built into the face of the Wall, the inscription written in Hebrew characters included the name 'Nahum' and the word 'Anno.' The stone is believed to have come from a Jewish tombstone of an early date, probably part of the haul of materials taken from the houses of Jews ransacked by the Barons for rebuilding the Wall in 1215.

In 1875, 75yds of the Wall forming this back enclosure to the hospital was demolished to widen what is now the London Wall thoroughfare, with much of the foundations, at least in 1937, surviving under the roadway. The east end of the original hospital site now lies under Finsbury Circus Gardens, originally known as 'Fensbury', another reference to the marshy nature of the land. It was here in October 1548 that the Great Protector, Edward Seymour, Duke of Somerset, was met and congratulated by the Lord Mayor, Aldermen and citizens of London on his return from defeating the Scots at the Battle of Pinkie Cleugh, which enabled the English to occupy south-eastern Scotland. When Henry VIII died in 1547, his son Edward was too young to rule and so Seymour was made Protector of the Realm. As well as determining war on Scotland he made changes to the Church of England, which included the introduction of the English Prayer Book and allowing members of the clergy to marry. He was also responsible for helping to raise the level of 'the Fen' at Moor Fields with hundreds of cartloads of bones removed from the charnel house of

St Paul's, hence the name Bonehill, now Bunhill Fields. As already touched upon, the level of the moor had been raised by 1606. That part along here to such an extent that it was laid out with elm trees and benches, creating London's first public park.

Another long stretch of London Wall before Finsbury Fields was demolished in 1817 when some handsome houses designed by the architect George Dance graced the rim of this arena-like open space, or circus. On other areas of higher, or sloping ground were poles with ropes stretched across them placed at intervals, upon which carpets and floor-covers were placed and beaten with such ferocity that 'it was expedient to hold your cambric or bandanna over your mouth and nostrils to avoid the clouds of dust'. This unwholesome industry notwithstanding, Finsbury Circus had become by the 1820s London's fashionable medical quarter, swarming 'with doctors and surgeons, who made large earnings out of the chiefs and prosperous business folk of the City.' But high rents due to the centralisation and development of commerce eventually forced the medical fraternity to move west, to the 'less socially deserted' districts of Cavendish Square and Harley Street. In 1900 the Corporation of London acquired Finsbury Circus by Act of Parliament, making this Grade II Listed garden the largest open space in the City. All that remains of Moor Fields, the present oval garden with its immaculate bowling green, home to the City of London Bowling Club, was originally laid out in 1815 to a design by Charles Dance. Surrounded by elegant curved terraces containing listed buildings, it is celebrated for its mature London plane trees (some over 200 years old), its bedding and fine Japanese Pagoda tree, the only one in the City.

Blomfield Street, in about the year 1636, saw another section of London's City Wall broken down to make way for a pedestrian gate. The bone-white premises in the corner of this street and London Wall is (at the time of writing) occupied by another fashionable restaurant, its sleek, clean lines in stark contrast to the battered stretch of decidedly grubby-looking brick wall following on. A small cast-iron tablet is hammered into the upper part of this wall of nineteenth-century London yellow stocks built on courses of earlier bricks of blood red. The plaque bears the date 1888, no doubt the year the wall was repaired and the letters A.H.W., for All Hallows-on-the-Wall.

A church is first mentioned on this site in 1120 in its connection with Holy Trinity Priory, Aldgate. Dedicated to All Hallows (or All Saints) the suffix 'on the wall' denotes the position of the church built into the City Wall on the original Roman foundations. Excavations in 1905 revealed that these consist of three courses, interlaid with tile and with the foundation extending down some 14 or 15ft below the present ground surface level, or the same height underfoot again as the more modern wall above ground. Built into the foundation is a Roman drain of tiles and similar to that visible in Noble Street. It is said that the drainage of the moors began to improve soon after the Romans left, by blocking these culverts cut into the City Wall and allowing for the flow of the Walbrook River. The body of the 50ft length of Wall surviving underground comprises interior and exterior faces of stone roughly squared and set in the red mortar associated with particularly wet areas, or where a longer setting time is required. At regular intervals of four and five courses of stone, triple courses of brick

40 Photograph of London Wall,
All Hallows-on-the Wall

carry right through the thickness of the Wall in the usual way, with the whole filled
with coarse rubble the consistency of concrete. Above ground where it meets the
church, the later brick wall gives way to ragstone, probably recycled Roman but of
medieval construction. Walter G. Bell records in 1937 the City's grime hanging 'thickly
on this short length of wall, giving it a dark and entirely unattractive appearance'.
Before the great clean up just a few short decades ago, the entire City was similarly
cloaked in the thick residue of a century and more of coal burning. That this same
coating has been allowed to remain on the face of this medieval Wall confers on the
grime the added status of an historical artefact in its own right.

Unlike most other City of London churches, All Hallows-on-the-Wall was
unaffected by the Great Fire and is one of the few buildings that remain of architect
and surveyor, George Dance the Younger, hailed as one of the most outstanding
architects of his time. The church was built between 1765 and 1767, replacing the
one built around 1300. Dance was only twenty-four years old when he took on the
commission. Like many a young man of the wealthy at the time he had recently
returned from his Grand tour of Italy where he conducted detailed studies of
Classical buildings, from which All Hallows takes its inspiration. Remarkably
simple in form with no aisles, its interior consists solely of a barrel-vaulted nave
and decoration deriving from the ancient Temple of Venus and Rome. Its exterior
is plain brick except for the Portland stone tower. The archaeological excavations
of 1905 also revealed that the half-dome apse on the City Wall side of the church
was determined by the foundations of a Roman bastion, thought to have been
added to the Wall for extra protection in the late third century AD. William Lethaby
visited the excavation and was able to declare the bastion 'certainly Roman'. Built
of random rubble, principally of irregular pieces and ragstone with portions of

Roman tile and other material, the base comprised large recycled square stones 2ft high, with several Lewis holes evidence of previous use. This base rested on a square table of large flat stones 9in thick, mostly comprising portions of a recycled cornice that protruded from the City Wall as much as 3ft on the eastern side. Gravel that was found in the intervening space was undisturbed. Roman origin was again determined by use of red mortar in foundations laid about 3ft below that of the City Wall and projecting into the original Roman ditch.

Approaching the church from the direction of Moorgate, it is just possible to see over the top of the wall to glimpse this semicircular protrusion. There is no public access to the slither of land between the north face of the Wall and the rear of premises in New Broad Street and therefore no means of studying this feature. Passing by one day, I found the church open and a volunteer busily taking photographs of the interior. Although it survived the Great Fire, All Hallows on-the-Wall was the first church to be burned by bombing during the Second World War. It was not fully restored for twenty years, by which time it had become a Guild Church, which means that it no longer has parish responsibilities, but more specialised functions. The ceiling is magnificent, a faithful restoration of Dance's original, the altar piece a copy of Berretini's Ananias restoring sight to Saint Paul, which was painted by Dance's brother, Nathanial. The floor is made up of Dance's original paving of white Portland stone and black marble. Part way down the nave there is a door on the left, which leads to the apse. I was told it is where the church vestments are kept (not on show to visitors), but was allowed to haul myself up onto the window ledge behind the font where it's possible to see the projection resting on foundations laid down by the Romans. Walter G. Bell notes in his pre-war observations that in order to reach his pulpit, the parson during Divine Service had to walk out of the church into the vestry and from there ascend steps to an opening in the Wall which gave the sole means of access.

Much like the bastion opposite St Giles' Cripplegate, so the one at All Hallows was a London Wall hermitage, perhaps the best known of all. In 1314, under the reign of Edward II, this 'tourelle [tower] on London Wall, near Bishopsgate,' was granted to Sir John de Elsyngham, chaplain, on condition that he maintained it and kept it in good repair, 'protected against wind and rain' and that he should 'properly behave himself'. This former fortification provided the ideal association of hermit's cell and its material connection with the church. It would have had perhaps two or three windows, the one considered most important opening into the church towards the altar allowing the recluse to witness the celebration of Mass. A second or third window knocked through the outer wall would have served for lighting the cell, receiving food and alms and for talking to visitors. There was an anchoress at All Hallows in 1459 who was succeeded by an anchorite, William Lucas, who died about 1486. The church accounts show these recluses not only as the recipients of charity but also as contributors. Money was given by Lucas for painting the church and Simon the Anker (author of a treatise called *The Fruit of Redemption*, printed in 1514) gave a stand of ale, contributed towards a new aisle, presented a silver chalice weighing 8oz and had his servant plaster the church wall. Other cells that could not be built against the outer church wall were arranged where a view of the interior was obtainable, perhaps in a chamber above the porch, or a space in the tower. Otherwise these recluses lived mostly a solitary life apart from the church, like the ones at St Giles. In the days of its role in civil defence, all encroachments about the City Wall were removed and no extension of property was allowed within at least sixteen feet of its inner face. Where they were built against the Wall, these hermit cells occupied just a few feet of land in odd corners, and given their purpose had little difficulty in obtaining relief from the civic law.

Number 55 London Wall was found in the first half of the twentieth century to rest on a length of City Wall measuring 43ft long and 12ft high, excavated 17ft below the modern level. Buildings on this north side of the thoroughfare were said to stand on the lower courses of the Roman wall, but where they stood (or stand) is now not clear to the passer by. The numbering of shops and offices has, alas, become a lost art. I walked into one major retailer along London Wall to check its number only to have the staff hunt high and low for a piece of headed notepaper with that information on it. Recent excavations confirm that the line of the Wall is preserved under the back walls of the shops and offices fronting on to Wormwood Street, built originally as a row of small buildings in the late seventeenth century. The City Wall was gradually replaced by brickwork, extending no further than the churchyard of St Botolph to the rear. An eighteenth-century plan of a shop in Wormwood Street offers a typical example. The frontage included the shop and a room measuring just over 24ft wide by 14ft deep. A staircase was built towards the rear of the premises leading up to a kitchen, a dining room and another room on the first floor, with two chambers and two garrets above. In 1887 Mr Loftus Brock reported to the British Archaeological Association the removal of part of the City Wall in Wormwood Street. In 1998, during the redevelopment of nos. 22–24, a section of Wall was examined by the Museum of London Archaeological Service, which threw up a theory that the Roman Wall was actually constructed largely of recycled materials. If so, then something in the region of half a million used bricks would have been required to build the 2-mile stretch and without any real study of this staple building material, there is no reason to suppose that the bricks discovered were any older than those used elsewhere. The Copperplate Map of 1553–59 shows the remains of another bastion tower situated about midway along Wormwood Street, although nothing is recorded of this from the excavation. The base of a Roman rubbish pit was excavated and two Roman wells were exposed, one of which was fully excavated, the other revealing some glass, pottery and animal bones. The north basement wall of 23–24 Wormwood Street is a Scheduled Ancient Monument consisting of foundations and some of the superstructure of the Roman city wall. Fragments of Roman tile were reused in footings for the post-medieval basement wall of 22 Wormwood Street. Despite their status it is not possible for members of the public to view these remains. Wormwood Street gives way to another major City thoroughfare that takes its name from a former gate where, at the time of writing, massive redevelopment is taking place for the new Heron Tower project, effectively a sunken island bounded by Camomile Street, Houndsditch and Bishopsgate.

41 Map from Bishopsgate to Aldgate

6

Bishopsgate to Aldgate

Bishopsgate as a City thoroughfare follows the alignment of the Roman road from the Basilica and Forum out of Londinium towards Lincoln and York. Gone is 110 Bishopsgate, a post-war concrete box typical of City office space in the 1960s, and with it the cast of a Bishop's mitre. Its counterpart survives on the upper face of Boot's the Chemist, on the corner of Wormwood Street and Bishopsgate. This gilded piece of high-ecclesiastical headgear marks the west end of the former City Gate. All of the learned sources reiterate John Stow's vagueness as to a firm association with this gate and the Bishops of London, although he does consider Erkenwald, the son of King Offa, and brother of Ethelburga to whom the tiny medieval Bishopsgate church, virtually destroyed by an IRA bomb in 1993, is dedicated. One piece of corroborative evidence I have yet to see associated with Bishopsgate is Bishop's Hall, now the site of the London Chest Hospital, close to Victoria Park on the boundary of Bethnal Green with Hackney. This 'palace' later became known as Bonner's Hall after Edmund Bonner, an especially notorious Bishop of London during the bloody reigns of Henry VIII and Queen Mary. William (a Norman), who was consecrated Bishop of London in the year 1051 to Edward the Confessor, held as the domain of the Bishopric the whole of what we know today as Tower Hamlets. Bishop's Hall was a retreat nestling on the western fringe of a vast hunting ground known as Bishopswood of which Epping Forest is the largest surviving expanse and Victoria Park the last fragment close to the City of London. Still extant is Bishop's Way, leading off the Cambridge Heath Road towards Victoria Park and the site of Bishop's Hall. Bishop Roger Niger is believed to have died there in 1241, likewise Bishop Baldock in 1313 and Ralph Stratford in 1355. Bishop Braybroke, who was Lord Chancellor, spent much of his time there until he died in 1404, after which there is no record of other resident Bishops except for Bonner between 1539 and 1549 who is said to have spent much time plotting beneath the ancient mulberry tree that survives in the grounds of the London Hospital, or torturing martyrs.

Erkenwald may well have restored the Roman gate in the seventh century as one of his many 'charitable Accounts' as Bishop of London. There were the effigies of two bishops on the gate in Stow's time, one probably Erkenwald and the other possibly Bishop William, another great benefactor, partly by his own goodness and partly by preserving the ample privileges enjoyed by the Bishops of London since 'before-time'. Bishopsgate served the City's transport needs primarily north and Aldgate further south served the east, although both converged. At Mile End travellers out of Aldgate could turn north towards Bethnal Green, passing Bishop's Way on the Cambridge Heath Road. The route out of Bishopsgate led directly to Shoreditch Church along what is today the A10, or by turning east at Shoreditch church onto what is today Hackney Road, crossing the Cambridge Heath Road for Bishop's Way.

Although there is little or no archaeological evidence for what the Roman gate looked like, it probably boasted the requisite twin towers flanking two entrance ways in common with the other Roman City gates. In the 1900s a mass of masonry was found within the line of the Wall, underlying what was thought substantially Roman work. Henry III in the thirteenth century confirmed to the Hansa merchants certain privileges by which they were bound to keep Bishopsgate in good repair, in exchange for using London as their base. The Hansa merchants were an alliance of foreign trading guilds that established and maintained a trade monopoly over the Baltic Sea, and to a certain extent the North Sea and most of Northern Europe until the seventeenth century. Their base, known as the Steelyard, was situated on the east bank of The Walbrook, which gave rise to the 'Steelyard privileges' they enjoyed. As early as 1272, however, it was found that their obligations regarding Bishopsgate were not being met, so a sizeable amount of compensation was granted to the Mayor and citizens of London for them and their successors to maintain the Gate. In 1346, Edward III granted Robert, the hermit of Bishopsgate, his protection for a year while collecting alms throughout England. Bishopsgate continued as a hermitage at least until 1426, when mention is made of a woman recluse living there, receiving 40s a year from the Sheriffs of London. The Hansa Merchants clearly back on track with regard to their agreed responsibilities, 'beautifully builded' the gate in 1479, presumably when these solitary lodgers moved out. In 1551 stones were being prepared for a new gate to be built when the Hanseatic League began to implode. The social and political changes that accompanied the Protestant Reformation and the rise of English merchants put an end to their special relationship with the City of London. Thus, Bishopsgate remained as familiar to John Strype in the 1700s as it was to John Stow a century and more previously. The carved effigies adorning the gate were probably the most ancient of any remaining in London, perhaps as old as the gate itself, which Strype calculated in his day to be more than 240 years. High up on each side survived the perceived effigies of the bishops William, 'the Conqueror's favourite', and Erkenwald, 'that lived near 400 Years before Bishop William, and was, for his Mortification and good Works, Sainted'. The figure on the east side was most likely that of William, sporting a long beard, his eyes sunk in an 'old mortified Face'. His mitre remained on his head but both his hands were either broken off or worn away by time. On the west side, over the cart passage, was the larger carving, probably that of Erkenwald, also complete with mitre and cloathed in his Pontificalibus. The crozier was broken off in his left hand, the right offering a blessing and the face described as 'smooth'. Either side of him were two even more ancient stone images. To the left a Saxon king, 'very probably King Alfred, who, after the Destruction of the City by Fire, and other Calamities of the People brought upon them by the Danes, restored and honourably repaired it'. The other figure appeared to represent some great nobleman, possibly Aeldred, Earl of Mercia, son-in-law to King Alfred.

The gate was rebuilt in its final form in 1735 but went the way of all the other City Gates in 1760–1. Prior to its destruction, the rooms over the gate were allotted for one of the Lord Mayor's carvers, who was also a Sergeant of the Chamber. As well as his eyewitness account of Bishopsgate before its demise, Strype leaves us an 'ingenious Account of these ancient Walls of London, and the Manner and Matter of their Building' courtesy of 'the Learned Dr Woodward', professor of Physics at Gresham College. In 1707, digging was taking place close to the Wall at Bishopsgate for the foundations of new houses and part of the demolished City Wall was being reused as hard core. This provided Dr Woodward with the perfect opportunity to study its fabric and composition. The foundation of the Wall he discovered lay 8ft beneath the present surface and from there upwards almost 10ft in height. Typical of its Roman construction, it mostly comprised ragstone interposed with single layers of broad tiles, each layer 2ft apart. The mortar (as expected) was very firm and hard, unlike the stone itself, which 'easily brake and gave away'. Even though the width from the foundation upwards measured 9ft, the Wall was not strong enough to withstand the demolition men who had it 'near levelled with the Ground'. Dr Woodward was able to confirm that the broad tiles were all of Roman make. Of the two sorts most commonly used, 'viz. Tegulae bipedales [2ft tiles] & sesquipedales' [18in tiles],' those he found were of the latter type, over an inch thick, 11in wide and over 17in long. He also found that the 'old Wall' having previously been demolished was repaired to a height of 8–9ft, possibly higher, built mostly of ragstone interposed with a few bricks. On the outside were layers of 5in-thick squared stone and between them alternate courses of very large brick. These he described as 'being of the Shape of the Modern; but Eleven Inches in Length, and Five in Breadth, and Two and a half in Thickness'. No tiles were used in these repairs, however, nor was the mortar as hard as that of the Roman builders. Still extant were the 2ft thick and 6ft high battlements and copings added in 1477 of the type surviving at St Alphage, using red and black brick as decoration. Also, the workmen found that they had to dig considerably lower than the foundations of the gate to reach the base of the old City Wall by as much as 4 or 5ft. Dr Woodward explained that as the level of the ground within the City had been successively raised by dint of waste across the ages, so the Wall without was required to be raised in proportion.

John Strype writes of a lane 13ft wide running from Aldgate to Bishopsgate between the Wall and the Priory of Holy Trinity, which had been stopped up with a wall of earth in the troublesome times of Henry III, another medieval monarch plagued by dissenting Barons. This defensive action was taken in the face of Henry's anger towards the City and remained in place for seven years. This action was judged to have disinherited the king of his highway, but nothing is known of the lane's restoration. Some remains either of the gate, or the Wall, or both, were uncovered between nos. 106 and 126 Bishopsgate in the early part of the twentieth century, now given way to the yawning Bishopsgate junction by Camomile Street, named after the fragrant herb said to have been grown outside the Wall to counter the whiff of the ripe City Ditch. The many unsuccessful attempts to prevent its becoming an open sewer have already been touched upon, but it is believed the number of dead dogs thrown into it at this point gave rise to the name of the road running parallel with Camomile Street, Houndsditch. Between the two in 1890, a 70ft stretch of City Wall was uncovered at the back of 31 Houndsditch, together with several pieces of memorial pillars decorated with a simple lattice pattern found in the remains of a bastion. More remains were found at the same time to the rear of Kempson House, which occupied 25–37 Camomile Street. In 1763 a drawing was made of a square tower, one of three thought to be Roman then standing in this area. It was built in alternate layers of massive square stones and red tiles with the old loophole for the sentinel enlarged into a square latticed window. More recent excavations along the southern frontage of Camomile Street and Bishopsgate have revealed severe disturbance by late nineteenth- and early twentieth-century basement building, and a feature interpreted as a possible piece of Roman City Wall foundation. This continued beyond the northern and eastern limits of the excavation, and not in a westerly direction as expected for the Wall, and so may either have been part of an earlier structure or an isolated foundation for the Wall, although no evidence of its superstructure has been found. In 2002 a cable trench crossed the line of the Roman and medieval City Wall at the junction of Bishopsgate and Camomile Street, just to the east of the site of the medieval gate house, but no trace of either monument was found. Of the archaeological features recorded were fragments of buildings earlier dated to before the late eighteenth century and evidence of the widening of Bishopsgate Street in 1971. Medieval remains consisted of one stone built fragment of pier base and two lengths of Wall foundation, one of which contained a relieving arch constructed of late fifteenth-century 'large bricks' made locally at Moorfields. This wall had been partly rebuilt in brick during the late eighteenth or early nineteenth century. An isolated brick foundation of eighteenth or early nineteenth century date completed the post-medieval remains.

Part of what remained of London Wall at the east end of Camomile Street was demolished in 1905 and the rest in 1926. The twenty-first-century Heron Tower construction site containing the whole of this area will eventually rise to over 200m and provide over 56,000 sq m of office floor space configured in three storey 'villages'. As well as over 600 sq m of shopping at the ground and basement levels, a sky-level restaurant is planned. The prediction and assessment of potential archaeological remains has become a well established consideration in the City of London planning process. Government guidance and policy in the City of London UDP aims to preserve in situ important archaeological remains, yet an evaluation carried out by the Museum of London between January and December 2006 prior to the development work, found very little surviving. Apart from several small finds, only traces of the notorious City Ditch were recorded, which, throughout its long and malodorous tenure had caused 'no small hindrance to the Canons of the Holy Trinity', whose great priory stretched from this point to Aldgate. A record of payment in 1519 for cleansing and scouring 'the common ditch' saw a chief ditcher paid 7*d* per day, a second ditcher 6*d*, the other ditchers 5*d* and every vagabond (or general labourer) 1*d*. With meat and drink thrown in, the charges to the City came in at just under £1000. Nine years later and it required cleansing again, this time at the expense of the Livery companies. In 1569, during the reign of Queen Elizabeth I, it was cleansed again and a new 'Sewer and Wharf of Timber' placed from the Tower at a cost of over £8000.

In 1876 a stretch of wall measuring 70ft was removed in Camomile Street together with the remains of a bastion, possibly the same as that later reported by William Lethaby in 1884. Among the discoveries was a carved limestone head (now lost), measuring 12.5in high representing an older man with a deeply furrowed forehead and cheeks, with short hair and beard characteristic of the middle third century. The size seems to indicate an imperial portrait or that of an important official. As far as Lethaby was aware, this bastion was the only example displaying any evidence of an attempt at bonding with the City Wall. Its foundations lay on two deep courses of heavy stones taken from Roman buildings, many sculptured and complete with the giveaway Lewis holes. These courses were set about 18in in front of the Wall, one over the other to form a straight joint, leaving a gap separated from the Wall by an intervening space filled with rubble and small stones similar to the arrangement found at All Hallows. This carefully arranged construction was designed to support the bastion away from the Wall and not lean inwards against it. It was also found that it incorporated a slope at the bottom of about 4ft. The masonry was described as ragstone rubble faced with random courses of facing blocks from 3–8.5in thick, and from 5–14in long. Lethaby was again on hand to confirm that the small facing blocks with concreted rubble were 'certainly Roman'. When this bastion was demolished, many sculptured stones from small but highly decorated edifices were found, leading the celebrated architectural historian to the conclusion that in the cemeteries surrounding Londinium there must have been mausoleum-like monuments of the kind common in the neighbourhood of Treves, the later Roman capital of Europe. After about AD 250 burial in coffins superseded the older form in individual or family tomb-houses. These were by no means uncommon in Britain, and usually square or circular. Some of the sculptured fragments found in the Camomile Street bastion were clearly parts of large scale sepulchral monuments, most measuring almost 4ft wide. One was over 3ft high with traces of a fine carved pattern. A large niche-head carved into an arch was possibly part of a monument containing a larger than usual figure of a man, the head of which was found at the same time. Two of the stones evidently came from angle pilasters of considerable scale, size and weight, indicating a monument comparable to those found near the City Gates of Rome. One fragment was of a naked boy, or Cupid, carrying a trident or a torch carved against a background of foliage on one side, with similar ornament on the other side but without the boy. Possibly the front face had several figures like a similar pilaster found at Treves. Also thrown up was the earliest known depiction of a Londoner in the form of a tombstone statue of a soldier-come-civil-servant, otherwise known as 'The Camomile Soldier'. The tombstone, which is now on display in the Museum of London, resembles Roman military tombstones found in the Rhineland and depicts a figure wearing a cloak and tunic, short hair and carrying a sword, the scabbard of which is of the Pompeii-type, undecorated with a terminal knob and guttering. The sword handle assembly is complete with familiar handguard, handgrip and pommel. In his left hand he holds a scroll and six writing tablets which indicate clerical duties, common among soldiers working for the military administration in London during the Roman period.

Writing in *The Builder* in 1881, a Mr Watkins describes excavating what he identified as 'the second bastion east of Bishopsgate' with a mass of architectural remains and fragments of sculptured stone from tombs and public buildings extending 18ft outward from the City Wall towards Houndsditch. Some of these stones were dressed and weighed from one hundredweight to as much as a ton and a half. Mr Watkins also observed a channel 15in deep by 18in wide, probably a drain. It was filled at some stage with concrete mixed with chalk and flint, probably when the bastion was built against the Wall, making the drain obsolete.

St Mary Axe, running off into the City after Camomile Street, is dominated by what has become one of new millennium London's most iconic additions earning the popular epithet 'The Gherkin' because of its three-dimensional oval shape. Officially 30, St Mary Axe, it is built on the site of the listed Victoria Baltic Exchange, the once traditional meeting place of merchants and sea captains in the City of London that moved to its new purpose-built centre in 1903. In 1992 an IRA bomb badly damaged the listed building, and in a controversial decision the planning application to replace it was passed on the grounds it would have been difficult to restore. And so, in 1994, the Baltic was forced to celebrate its 250th anniversary in a new home. Exactly a century prior to that decision no such controversy surrounded the clearing of London's built landscape. A further 25ft of London Wall and a bastion containing several sculptured stones at the junction of St Mary Axe with Camomile Street was cleared with ease. Long before elected ministers were required to take an interest in such matters, this loss was consigned to the pages of a paper published by the London and Middlesex Archaeological Society as a matter of fact, not regret. Similarly in 1913 when another 120ft section of London Wall was uncovered and then demolished in Bevis Marks. On the wall

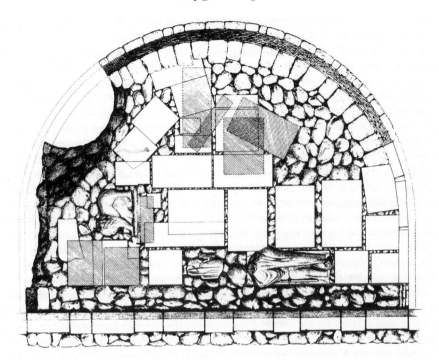

42 Plan of Camomile Street bastion recorded in 1876

of numbers 10–16 is a surviving Museum of London plaque, which explains that although the City Wall has now gone, the street pattern remains basically the same. *The Builder* for 28 May 1887 reports the discovery of another semicircular bastion foundation opposite this spot, which like most of the others found on this eastern stretch was not bonded into the City Wall and contained reused stones. The fact that it contained more coping-stones than could have been obtained from the portion of parapet wall destroyed when the bastion was built, offers up the notion that other elements, such as the original internal turrets, were modified during the construction of the bastions. A small figure was found, probably a grave monument, of either Atys (a God whose death and resurrection symbolised the end of winter and the arrival of spring), or Silvanus (God of fields and woods and flocks). The small courtyard off 10–12 Bevis Marks contains Britain's oldest synagogue and one of the best-preserved houses of worship of its period still in regular use. It occupies the site of the City mansion and gardens of the abbots of Bury, or 'Bury's Marks', hence Bevis Marks. A Jewish quarter in London is first mentioned in 1128, although believed to have been present since at least from the time of the Norman Conquest. Jewry Street in the heart of London's financial centre was where Jews settled both before their expulsion in 1290 and after resettlement 350 years later. Following the petitioning for settlement in England in 1656, synagogues were built in Creechurch Lane, Duke's Place and Bevis Marks, of which only the latter survives. Built in 1701 the synagogue was established to serve the Spanish and Portuguese Jewish community. Despite recent restoration, the interior, built in the style of a Nonconformist chapel of the period, with a touch of Sir Christopher Wren in evidence, has barely changed. It has one of the finest collections of Cromwellian and Queen Anne furniture in the country and magnificent brass candelabra. The day I visited, the man on duty knew nothing more than this. He had never heard of the London Wall, only the one in China and the one in Berlin, which he thanked God was now no more. I told him that I had read somewhere that fragments of Roman bastion masonry survived in the foundations of the synagogue. 'Walls are about division,' he said, 'we are better off without them.' The fine-looking building appears to stand too far from the route of the Wall for either it or the bastion to have been incorporated into its foundations. 'But who really knows about these things?' the man in black shrugged. 'To confirm it we would have to open the ground, and this we cannot do.' I said I understood and went on my way.

Bevis Marks merges into Duke's Place where the slight curve of the road is dictated by the line of the ancient fortification. Duke's Place was formerly part of the priory of Holy Trinity, founded by Queen Maud, the wife of King Henry I, in the year 1108. In order to establish the foundation, the four parishes of St Mary Magdalen, St Michael, St Catharine and the Blessed Trinity, were united in the one parish of the priory of the Holy Trinity called Christ Church. Initially the church was built on a modest piece of land. Over time it expanded enormously to surpass all other priories in the City of London, or indeed the county of Middlesex. It was dissolved in 1531 when it was granted by Henry VIII to Sir Thomas Audley who had spoken against Cardinal Wolsey. Afterwards Lord Chancellor, Audley created a noble mansion from the priory. His only daughter was married to Thomas, Duke of Norfolk, to whom the estate passed, giving us Duke's Place. Thomas, however, lost his head on Tower Hill and the mansion passed to Thomas Howard, Earl of Suffolk, the eldest son. It was eventually sold to the City Corporation and thereby the citizens of London, 'to have and to hold to them and their successors'. There is nothing to see of this generous legacy today, although archaeological excavations in the 1970s did reveal a doorway which had been cut through the City Wall and blocked up in the fifteenth century. This was thought to have provided access to properties owned by the Priory outside the City Wall. As the bottom of the doorway revealed, the ground level had already risen 7ft by the medieval period.

A late Roman date for the bastion here was found by Peter Marsden in 1971. The foundation had been dug through an earlier deposit containing fourth-century material, and was overlaid by a later and thicker layer of refuse containing pottery with nothing recognisably later than coins dated to AD 364–75. These deposits having accumulated after the bastion was built, as the evidence suggests, fits with the theory that the bastions were added to the City Wall as part of General Theodosius' programme of reconstruction in AD 369. When uncovered this bastion stood more than 3ft high and contained a number of large sculptured stone blocks, although time constraints did not allow for the complete excavation required to produce conclusive dating evidence. Also discovered was a length of early camp ditch with evidence to suggest that it was filled in soon after it was dug, raising the possibility of the site of Londinium's first Roman fort. The ditch comprised what Ralph Merrifield graphically describes as an 'ankle-breaking gully' at the bottom, typical of military V-shaped ditch. It ran in a north-easterly alignment from Aldgate High Street, the former Roman highway connecting Londinium with Camulodunum. Another piece of evidence indicating the presence of a fortified enclosure was a bone handle-grip from a Roman legionary sword.

Excavations in 1977 for the subway running under Duke's Place cut through the actual line of the City Wall, revealing Roman and medieval stonework. This passage of history is nicely depicted in a mosaic lining the subway wall under Duke's Place. The floor level is that of Roman and medieval. The height of the earth bank built up against the inside of the City Wall is shown to have risen about 6ft, with the subway ceiling representing a point just below waist height in medieval times. The modern street level is about 5ft above the height of the ceiling and half as much again was the Roman sentry walk and battlements. The subway entrance is in St James' Passage, at the rear of the Sir John Cass's Foundation C of E Primary School built in 1909.

Representing one of London's oldest and largest education charities, the foundation was started in 1748 with money bequeathed by the Will of Sir John Cass and supports educational opportunities for young people from disadvantaged backgrounds who live in inner London, and also makes grants available to schools, organisations and other educational establishments. John Cass was born in the City of London in 1661 and served as both Alderman and Sheriff and Member of Parliament for the City. Knighted in 1713, three years earlier he had set up a school for fifty boys and forty girls in the churchyard of St Botolph-without-Aldgate. He intended to leave all his property to the school, but died suddenly in 1718 without completing his Will. His wishes were finally upheld thirty years after his death when the school was reopened and the famous City Foundation established. Attached to the school's north wall is the Museum of London plaque Number 5. On it is an artist's impression of the Roman gate built into the City Wall that straddled the Roman road that today takes its name, Aldgate.

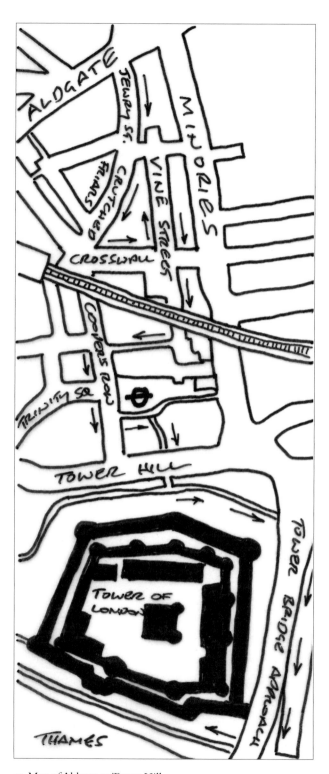

43 Map of Aldgate to Tower Hill

7

Aldgate to the Tower

Roman in origin, the earliest documentary record for Aldgate is from a plan of Holy Trinity made in 1592, which indicates a single road passageway with pedestrian access both sides flanked by two large semicircular towers. The map clearly shows one half of this configuration and also reveals that the inner face of the Wall had been cut away from this point as far west as the bastion facing Bevis Marks synagogue. This had the effect of increasing the 15ft inner passageway by as much as 5ft. What were believed to be parts of the Gate foundations were uncovered in 1907 on the south side of Aldgate High Street, 25ft east from the corner of Jewry Street at a depth of 16ft. A year later and similar remains were uncovered on the north side under the former Post Office. The level of these remains suggests Roman foundations, although the only conclusive evidence there is lies in the line of the City Wall and the thoroughfare itself, built to link Londinium with the old Roman capital of Camulodunum (Colchester). Without much to go on in the way of archaeological and documentary evidence, it's likely that much of the Roman Gate remained intact for several centuries. Aldgate is mentioned in Canute's reign (1016–35) and may have been rebuilt early in the twelfth century by the Prior of Holy Trinity when a grant by Matilda dated to 1108 records it as 'Portam de Alegate'. Aldgate also shares the same distinction with Newgate in affording the Barons entry into London in 1215. As Strype relates:

> Having then also secret Intelligence, that they might enter the City of London, if they would, they removed their Camp to Ware, from whence in the Night coming to London they entered Aeldgate, and placing Guardians or Keepers of the Gates, they disposed of all Things in the City at their Pleasure. They spoiled the Fryars Houses, and searched their Coffers; which being done, Robert Fitzwater, Jeffrey Magnavile, Earl of Essex, and the Earl of Gloucester, chief Leaders of the Army, applyed all diligence to repair the Gates and Walls of this City, with the Stones taken from the Jews broken Houses; namely, Aeldgate, being then most ruinous, (which

had given them an easy Entry) they repaired, or rather newly builded, after the manner of the Normans, strongly Arched, with Bulwarks of Stone brought from Cane in Normandy, and small Brick, called Flanders Tile, was brought from thence, such as hath been here used since the Conquest, and not before.

The accommodation above the gate consisted of various dwelling rooms and there was a cellar on the south side. The celebrated English poet Geoffrey Chaucer lived here from 1374 when appointed a government official at the Port of London, holding the post of Comptroller of the Customs and Subside of Wools, Skins, and Tanned Hides. *Monk's Tale* was published the same year while busy writing arguably his most abiding tome, *Canterbury Tales*. On the understanding he was not to be disturbed, only 'in time of defence of the City when the authorities might re-enter', Chaucer undertook the obligation of the gate's maintenance and repair. He also received a pledge that the gate would not be used as a gaol during his lifetime, narrowly escaping incarceration himself when charged with rape, but his guilt or innocence has never been determined. He had been married for over ten years to Philippa Roet, a lady-in-waiting in the queen's household and the couple were thought to have had three or four children together. Philippa's sister, Katherine Swynford, later became the third wife of John of Gaunt, the king's fourth son and Chaucer's patron. His first narrative poem, *The Book of the Duchess*, was written shortly after the death of Blanche, Duchess of Lancaster, first wife of John Gaunt, in September 1369. Chaucer had begun writing *The House of Fame* when, in 1385, he lost his job and rent-free home and moved to Kent where he was appointed as justice of the peace and was later elected to Parliament.

During the reign of Edward IV (1399–1483) Aldgate once again 'felt maces beat at its doors' in the concluding scene to the long, drawn-out Wars of the Roses. Indicative of the manner in which the Civil War divided families, the illegitimate son of William Neville, Thomas, Lord Fauconberg, otherwise 'the Bastard of Fauconberg' (Falconberg, Falconbridge or Faucomberge), supported the Lancastrian Henry VI, while his father stood for the Yorkist Edward IV. Richard Neville, the Earl of Warwick, aka 'The Kingmaker' fell at the Battle of Barnet in April 1471 and a month later the Battle of Tewkesbury quashed the hopes of the Lancastrians. Unaware of these events, Thomas presented himself at the head of a 17,000-strong force at the gates of London Bridge, stating his intention to dethrone the usurper Edward and restore King Henry. He asked permission to march through London, claiming he held a commission from the Earl of Warwick as Vice-Admiral, only to learn that he had been dead nearly three weeks. Fauconberg refused to accept this news and continued in his demand to pass through London. The Mayor and Aldermen asked him to lay down his arms and acknowledge Edward, who was now firmly established as king, but Fauconberg refused and the siege of London began. Three thousand of his men divided into two companies for an attack on Bishopsgate and Aldgate while Fauconberg concentrated on London Bridge. The siege on Bishopsgate failed dismally and the company despatched to Aldgate. They managed to break through, only to have the portcullis brought down on them whereupon they were slaughtered to a man. Alderman Robert Basset, in charge at Aldgate, then ordered his citizen army to open the gate and 'in God's name, and, by a brave sortie', forced the attackers back. Caught between reinforcements from the Tower, the rebels were driven as far east as Stratford. Some 700 of them were killed and many hundreds taken prisoner and held to ransom. Fauconberg eventually handed over his fleet of 56 ships to King Edward, who pardoned him. Four months later, however, and Fauconberg was taken prisoner and executed. His and the heads of nine comrades were stuck on spears and put on display around London, 'till the elements and the carrion crows had left nothing of them there but the bones.'

Aldgate had its hermitage, a small projecting turret built into the City Wall on the south side of the gate measuring about 4ft onto the king's highway. Decreed in the reign of Edward I, John the Hermit was resident in 1257–8, during which time he had built the cell overlooking the large cemetery that had grown up outside the City Wall begun by the Romans. Queen Mary passed through Aldgate on 3 August 1555 when she made her first entry into London from Norfolk. She was greeted in part by the boys of the newly-founded Christ's Hospital. John Howes, clerk to Richard Grafton, the first Treasurer General of the Hospital, describes the stage set up outside Aldgate upon which were placed the Mayor, Aldermen and the children of 'the free schoole'. One of the boys had prepared an oration to greet the Queen, but she passed by the stage deliberately ignoring the child. Writing some forty-five years after the event, Grafton explains that the Queen's behaviour openly displayed her opinion of the Reformation, exhibiting her dislike of the 'the blewboys' whose school displaced the Greyfriars.

The last great procession to pass under the Aldgate was the funeral in 1587 for the celebrated poet, courtier and diplomat, Sir Philip Sidney, who died at the age of thirty-two from wounds he received fighting the Spanish at Zutphen, on his uncle the Earl of Leicester's expedition. To many of his contemporaries, Philip Sidney represented the ideal of the renaissance courtier who became one of the most influential Elizabethan poets. His body was taken from a house in the Minories where it had been left for several months due to a lack of funds to carry out the funeral, the cortege passing into the City through Aldgate led by 23 poor men and 700 gentlemen on foot, followed by his regiment of cavalry, the Lord Mayor and 300 Trained Bands. Lack of funds had taken its toll on the gate, too, which was by this time 'very old and ruinous'. On his entry into London in 1606, King James I gave the Mayor £300 for gifts to the poor and the rebuilding of Aldgate. Demolition began shortly after and in the process produced many Roman artefacts. One of the surveyors of the work, Mr Martin Bond, had two of the Roman coins found carved in stone 'according to their true Form and Figure' and fixed either side of the east arch. The rest of the hoard was handed over to the Mayor and Aldermen at the Guildhall. On 10 April, 1607, Mr Bond laid the first foundation stone of the new gate, the bottom of the foundation being 16ft deep and 8ft wide, and much in-keeping with the remains that would be dug up by workmen exactly 300 years later.

The work was 'substantially and famously' finished in 1609. On the top of the gate, on the east side, stood a golden sphere complete 'with a goodly Vane on it', and on the upper battlements were placed the statues of two Roman soldiers as sentinels, each holding a stone ball in defiance of any enemy of the City. Beneath them in a large square stood the figure of James I in gilt armour and at his feet, a golden lion supporting England and a chained unicorn for Scotland, both displaying the necessary 'Awe and Humility in the Presence of so great a Person'. On the west side of the gate, standing 'highest of all,' was the gilded figure of Fortune standing upon a mound or a globe, with 'a prosperous Sail spreading over her Head, and looking gracefully upon the City'. Beneath her and in another large square was the King's Arms richly carved with the motto DIEU ET MON DROIT, and below VIVAT REX. Somewhat lower, 'and to grace each Side of the Gate', were two female figures, one the emblem of Peace with a dove in one hand and a gilded wreath or garland in the other, and the other on the north side over a pedestrian Postern the figure of Charity with a child at her breast and another in her hand, implying, 'that where Peace and Love and Charity do prosper, and are truly embraced, that City shall be for ever blessed'.

Queen Marie de Medici made her State entry into London through Aldgate in 1638 on her way to pay a visit to her daughter Queen Henrietta Maria. And a month before the Great Fire of London was to fill the pages of his famous diary, Samuel Pepys passed through Aldgate returning from a 'noble supper' at Lady Pooley's house in Bow. At 'Allgate' he was stopped to ascertain if he was with his wife or 'a common courtesan', for Aldgate had the dubious distinction as a haunt of rogues, vagabonds and ladies of the night. An early City Ordinance decreed that: 'If any woman shall be found to be a common courtesan, and if the same shall be attainted, let her be taken from the prison unto Algate, with a hood of ray, and white wand in her hand; and from thence with minstrels, unto the thew [a kind of pillory] and there let the cause be proclaimed.' And there were harsher penalties too, which were in force until the eighteenth century. In 1714, at the height of rumours about a Jacobite rising, an outspoken Tory schoolmaster called Boulnois was flogged from the Stock Market to Aldgate where he died.

Ten years later, and 115 years after it had been 'beautified', Daniel Defoe noted on his *Tour Through the Island of Great Britain* that Aldgate 'was very ancient and decay'd', hence the adage 'as old as Aldgate'. But, according to the businessman, soldier, economic journalist and spy, it still looked very well, although one of the Roman soldiers had thrown down his stone 'after having held it upwards of an hundred years; but, as it happened, it did no harm'. The gate at this time was temporarily used as a debtors' prison during the rebuilding of the Poultry debtors' gaol which was destroyed in the Great Fire. It lasted only another thirty-five years before it was removed along with all the other gates to free up the roads to ease the flow of trade. Aldgate was purchased by a Mr Mussell of Bethnal Green, described as a 'zealous antiquary'. He inhabited a large house belonging to Lord Viscount Wentworth, built in the reign of James II, onto which he attached the gate on the north side renaming it Aldgate House. There was a bas-relief on the south face said to have been carved from Watt Tyler's tree, an ancient oak on Bow Common, which the City Council had carved. Aldgate House, together with the remnants of the old City Gate, was itself demolished in 1806.

Across Aldgate from Sir John Cass's Foundation C of E Primary School is Jewry Street, a reference to the Jewish community who resettled just inside the City Gates after almost four centuries of expulsion from England as a result of the Crusades. In 1861 another considerable stretch of City Wall was uncovered on the east side during building works. The remains of two more bastions were also uncovered towards the end of that century. The imposing red-brick confection we see today was built in 1899 to the design of A.W. Cooksey for the newly founded Sir John Cass Technical Institute, which moved into its new premises in 1902. The Institute changed its name to the Sir John Cass College in 1950 and in 1965 merged with the Central School of Art to form the Sir John Cass School of Art in Whitechapel. Its Department of Navigation merged with part of the King Edward VII Nautical College in 1969 and moved to a new building at Tower Hill. The college then combined with the City of London College in 1970 to create the City of London Polytechnic that has subsequently become the London Metropolitan University. When the building was extended in 1934, evidence of the City Ditch was found sloping down to a depth of about 30ft below the present ground level, and an evaluation carried out by the Museum of London in December 1991 discovered that only the foundation and sandstone plinth survived. Traces of an east–west ragstone and mortar foundation abutting the Wall foundation on its outer side almost certainly belonged to the bastion identified by Ralph Merrifield in 1965, although it was not possible to establish its full extent or shape.

And so it was with these images in mind that I was led down into the basement of 31, Jewry Street to see the preserved remains. Through a forest of dexion shelving loaded with cardboard boxes, my guide stopped at a cupboard about 3ft off the ground. The glass door was opened to reveal a chunk of Roman Wall measuring perhaps 4ft high and about 2.5ft thick. Its outer face rests hard against a wall of black glazed Victorian wall tiles, while the inner face occupies a void of a few inches. Of the pair of ancient curling cardboard labels sometime attaching the piece, the upper one identifies 'Roman Tiles' and the other that what we are looking is a 'Portion of the Roman Wall (*in situ*)'.

'There's more,' I was glad to hear and was taken in a northerly direction following the line of the Wall to the end of another box-strewn corridor and a small utility area where, against the flickering hum of a neon light was exposed another cupboard, smaller than the first and about 5ft off the ground, containing a stub of Roman Wall. It is no bigger than a gas meter and is there as an example of the upper part of the Roman Wall, which presumably continues beyond the building's foundations.

I can only conclude that the archaeological evaluation which took place in 1991 was carried out elsewhere, as these remains bear little evidence of any disturbance for quite some considerable time. The Workplace Support Supervisor

44 Photograph of London Wall remains 3, Jewry Street (east)

who kindly showed me these fragments said that he receives a number of requests each year from people wanting to come and see them. 'One man came all the way from the Isle of Wight', he told me.

Number 2 Crutched Friars, offers an altogether different experience. This road takes its name from the House of the Friars of the Holy Cross – otherwise Crouched or Crossed, the middle English form of the word 'Cross' being 'Crouche' from the Latin 'Crux', hence Crutched Friars. They came to England in about 1248 and stayed briefly in London before settling in Oxford. The position

45 Photograph of London Wall remains 3, Jewry Street (west)

of the house for the thirteen student friars is not known. Stow has the street more generally known as Hart Street and he uses the name 'Crowched Friers' to denote a house there. Strype, however, maintains that it was more commonly called 'Crutched Fryers', which he deemed to be the proper designation. Sixty-five feet of Wall was found here during building work in 1904, of which only a fraction survived demolition or incarceration. In 1936 Walter G. Bell was granted permission to see what remained, which he declared to be 'an excellent and characteristic length of the wall'.

46 Photograph of Roman Wall in the cellar of Roman Wall House, No 1 Crutched Friars in 1936

Fifteen years later, and visiting the same, Norman Cook concurred. Bell imagined the sacrifice of space to preserve it was down to 'an enlightened builder', or perhaps it was the Saddler's Company responsible for the development. Possibly it was retained to reflect the name of new development dubbed Roman Wall House, as a unique selling point. Today a sheet of toughened glass protects it from those enjoying 'some serious downtime' in the Departure Bar, a modern club and bar of the type that has transformed the City's nightlife in recent years. Exquisitely displayed like a museum piece, the piece of Wall is set in an entirely contemporary experience, appropriately basking in the Imperial Red décor as almost a backdrop to the general spirit of new millennium bacchanalia.

About 8–9ft in height, it shows the first triple bonding course above the foundation, then four courses of squared ragstone, a triple bonding course with offset, six courses of ragstone and a double bonding course. Bell's description of the inner face being 'so perfect in condition' was probably down to the characteristic earth bank raised against it as soon as it was built, which had protected it. 'Ages old, the buried wall still does citizen service', observed Walter Bell. 'For along its line, dozens of City houses have been built directly upon it as a foundation – and none better could be desired'. Today it's a matter of crossing that line, quite literally, along Crosswall, which connects Crutched Friars and Vine Street, where a run of Wall and the foundation of a bastion were found by John Maloney of the Museum of London in 1980. It was squarer in plan and composed of layers of

47 Photograph of Roman Wall in the Departure Bar, Roman Wall House, No 1 Crutched Friars

ragstone, flints and lumps of *opus signinum* embedded in gravel and capped with rammed chalk. The foundation, which was 4ft in depth, was stepped down in two stages into the bottom of the ditch. These substantial remains were preserved and displayed beneath a glass viewing panel to the rear of 35, Vine Street. The home of leading law firm, Field Fisher Waterhouse, I was initially told that repair work was underway to the panel and so it wasn't possible to see the remains. I was, however, offered a piece of headed paper and asked to write or telephone for an appointment, which I found a little confusing. The day I eventually secured access it all became clear. It was raining hard and I presumed that I would need my umbrella, but instead of being taken outside, my escort led me to the lift and two storeys down to the level of Roman London. The brilliantly lit corridors with windowless rooms proved more cheery than the gloomy daylight outside. Past catering galleys and conference rooms we entered a large expansive chamber at least 30ft high and 50ft in length, and containing for the most part the most magnificent fragment of London's ancient City Wall preserved underground after that below the Merrill Lynch HQ. In its size and manner of presentation, this 32ft chunk is arguably even more impressive.

What is laid out is the exterior face of the Wall complete with its red sandstone plinth supporting regular courses of ragstone facings containing a rubble and mortar core bonded with tile. It rises to the ceiling where natural daylight filters through gaps in the tarpaulin laid to stem leaks in the glass observation panel.

48 Photograph of Roman Wall remains Emperor House 35, Vine Street

'Visitors used to be allowed to view the remains, but now they need to make an appointment' I was told. Again, it is important to remember that this is a business premises. Obligations aside, a member of staff has to be allocated to accompany visitors and that can't be arranged on the spot. I was grateful for the leaky panel otherwise I might never have got to see these remains as they need to be seen.

Evidence was also found of the V-shaped defensive ditch some 16ft wide, with the earth from this used to form a supporting bank on the inner side of the Wall. The ditch was later filled and a larger one dug further away from the Wall. The bastion foundations are contained in a modern brick revetment best viewed from the restaurant level, although that was not an option.

The bastion dates back to the troubled years of the later fourth century when extra fortifications were added. The importance of this find lies in the fact that it demonstrates that the eastern bastions were regularly spaced along the Wall, at intervals of about 180ft. Standing at about 30ft high, with a platform for heavier weaponry, the surviving foundations contained a typical mixture of ragstone, crushed chalk and recycled tombstones stepped into the earlier ditch to prevent subsidence. One such fragment was a monument stone dedicated to Marciana, aged ten. 'We're thinking about doing something with it,' my escort told me, referring to the remains of Wall and bastion, not the monument. Meanwhile, the piles of photocopy paper, cardboard boxes and old desks might be visually disagreeable, but not necessarily offensive. Rather, there is something very reassuring about such tangible human activity expressing the same disregard for the Wall shown

49 Photograph of bastion foundations Emperor House 35, Vine Street

by Londoners since the Romans left. The only truly irksome moment for me was the girl with a strong South African accent calling loudly to her colleagues that 'a tourist had got in' and was taking pictures of 'that wall'.

The 'tourist' continued south from Vine Street into America Square, flanked either side by the Minories and Fenchurch Street Station. During more extensive developments of the nineteenth century, other fragments of Roman Londinium were uncovered hereabouts just 9ft under the surface, such as tile used in the City Wall that varied from bright red to a pale yellow. The foundations and lower portions of Roman Wall found buried to a depth of about 20ft were destroyed during the building of the railway in 1841. When nos. 15 and 16 America Square were pulled down in 1908 a further 65ft of London Wall was similarly stripped away, including what remained of two more bastions variously discovered either side of Crosswall (then John Street), Chain Alley and Gould Square, themselves consigned to history. Along the south face of the railway bridge is a blind, unnamed passageway that provides rear access to various businesses. Next to it is another passage, again unnamed (but by no means blind) and beyond that, Crescent, a pleasing sweep of revival Georgian town houses planted immediately outside the limit of the City Wall.

The Revd P.B. 'Tubby' Clayton was appointed Vicar of All Hallows by the Tower in 1922 by the then Archbishop of Canterbury, Randall Davidson, with the intention of establishing a base for the development of Dr Clayton's continuing work as Founder Padre of Toc H. The Tetley Trust was established in 1931 with

Mrs Charlotte Tetley purchasing the freehold of 41, Trinity Square as that base and residence of the clergy of All Hallows. Money raised was to be used to maintain the house and for all charitable purposes in connection with the parish of All Hallows or with Toc H. The Wakefield Trust was established six years later with Lord Wakefield and 'Tubby' Clayton two of the original nine Trustees. Lord Wakefield presented the Trust with more houses in the vicinity to be used 'for such charitable purposes as will be most conducive to the development of Tower Hill and Trinity Square as a centre of welfare work or as a centre from which welfare work can be conducted'. The surrounding neighbourhood was defined as the City of London plus the area within a 1-mile radius of 41 Trinity Square. Numbers 42 and 43 Trinity Square variously housed the Tetley Trust hostel and the Toc H Club with at least nos. 6 to 8, Crescent included in the property portfolio. In January 2008, both Trusts merged to form the Wakefield & Tetley Trust. Although Trinity Square sits within the City limits defined by London Wall and Crescent without, this demarcation was at one time lifted when either no 6, Crescent or no 7, where Dr Clayton lived, was united with 42 Trinity Square.

In November 1936 Walter G. Bell took a photograph from this 'City Parson's back window'. The view was of the most complete section of City Wall still preserved other than St Alphage.

At 110ft long and standing to a height of 32ft above the original ground level, it then represented the north face of a warehouse belonging to Messrs. Barber & Co. Following in his footsteps in 1951, six years after the intervening World War,

50 Photograph of the external face of London Wall as part of Barber's Bonded Warehouse, Cooper's Row, Tower Hill in 1936

Norman Cook describes approaching the Toc H Club 'just north of Trinity Square' where in the basement a fragment of City Wall of about 30ft in length was excavated in 1938. Small parties were allowed to visit this relic 'by courtesy of the warden' and 'only if permission is asked', and not after 6 pm or on weekends, as it formed the north wall of Club sitting room. It was well worth making the effort, he enthused, if only for the descent to this lower level which offered 'an admirable idea of the way in which the ground level had risen since Roman times'. The section of London Wall seen here was the external face, showing the moulded plinth, four courses of ragstone, a triple bonding of red tiles and then six more courses of squared stone. Above this was more modern building work that carried the wall to ceiling height. That it was the exterior face of the Roman Wall exposed puts this basement room not in Trinity Square, but Crescent. Indeed, Norman Cook describes the front door of the Toc H building leading out into Crescent, confirming that the properties of both Trusts were once interlinked across the boundary of the City Wall.

Cook's purpose in all of this was like that of Bell, to catch sight of 'the most complete section of wall still preserved.' For some reason he didn't enjoy the view out of the vicar's rear window, but instead stood on a traffic island in the middle of the road to peer over the top of no 8, Crescent, which had lost its top storey through bombing. From that vantage point he was able to glimpse a fragment of medieval masonry topped by modern brickwork. Walter G. Bell found it difficult to believe that such a length of old City Wall survived intact, complete with sentry walk and protecting bulwark. At that time few knew of it. 'None of the half million people who pass in and out of the City every day has ever seen it,' he writes, 'or even heard of its existence – none save some archaeologists'. Bell was given a tour by one of the partners who echoed the sentiment of his great grandfather: 'why waste a good wall?' When the warehouse was being planned, the builder wondered what to do with the huge slab, 'immensely thick and hard as iron', and so rather than attempt the costly task of demolition he retained it. With a few shallow windows added at the bulwark level and a course or two of brick, the warehouse roof was sprung from the top and so was saved the most complete fragment of London Wall. By the flickering light of an oil lamp, that he 'might explore its intricacies', Bell passed under an arch cut through the thick Wall and into the building, ascending a steep stairway where bright electric lighting took over to illuminate the edifice 'in all its rugged mass'. As it headed due south towards the Tower of London the Wall no longer enclosed an entire City but one side of a wine vault. The height of over 20ft made for an imposing sight even though its true elevation was hidden beyond the rafters of the roof. Towards the top a medieval archer's loophole was clearly visible, which in more recent times had been glazed. The glass, however, had soon 'toned to a dirty yellow, through which penetrates a little of London's gloom… It seems absurd to call these dismal beams daylight', observed Bell. The larger stones making up the interior face of the Wall were covered in a velvety moss after decades of exposure to the fumes given off by the wines. 'Either the moss grew black or took the grime of the City'.

51 Photograph of the external face of London Wall, Cooper's Row, 2008

Below ground in the basement Bell found himself 'in a bit of Roman London, with the wall as the Roman builders left it'. He traced the bonding courses of tile in the wall, scratching away at the fungus to bring out the deep red colour, although a shallow test pit had been dug a few feet down 'at the instance of some antiquaries,' to examine the lower parts of the structure. The prolific chronicler of London history was left in no doubt that the loose sand and gravel marked the very bottom of the Wall. Making his way to the top was a climb of 35ft where the Wall was preserved like nowhere else in London. The stone and chalk represented the structure older than the repairs in 1477 when the battlements where replaced by brick. The sentry walk was complete with a protecting bulwark breast high and Bell was able to walk its length, considering the view when the Wall protected a London of narrow streets and red-tiled roofs and with green fields beyond. The same view in 1936 was limited to a mass of grimy brick walls, slate roofs and smoking chimney pots in all directions, an image that has now also become history. 'Tubby' Clayton resigned as vicar in 1962, but continued living at no 7 until his death in December 1972, just after his eighty-seventh birthday. The house was then used to provide accommodation for young Bangladeshi men recently arrived in Britain until this whole area was redeveloped in the 1980s.

That same mass of Wall explored by Walter Bell is now fully accessible and requires no written permission to see it. Leaving Crescent back in the direction of the railway arch, the passage to the left opens onto a world dominated by this massive relic now standing in splendid isolation, entirely free of any additions, rising to its thirty-five feet height and refusing to be diminished by the mixed cluster of more contemporary constructions about it. Only at its north end is it partially compromised by a column of shiny black granite supporting one corner of the Grange City Hotel, while its southern end is now fully exposed, gouging a division between Crescent and Trinity Square. The lower sections of the Roman construction once buried in basements are now preserved in a pit 15ft below the modern street level.

Passing under what is in all probability the same ragged arch mentioned by Walter G. Bell seventy years ago is no longer to enter a musty of world of grime-caked walls, but a sophisticated twenty-first century al fresco eating area where diners can enjoy authentic Japanese cuisine against the backdrop of this awesome slab of ancient London history. The characteristic red tile and ragstone construction is evident, as is where the Wall was heightened during the medieval period with irregular masonry narrowing to a sentry walk a precarious 3ft wide. Wooden stairs once led to this later addition, probably reached by a platform keyed into the socket holes visible below the loopholes where archers would have stood to deal out their lethal volleys. Norman Cook thought these openings dated from late Norman times, the larger one on the left now free of its dirty yellow glass and recognisable to the first medieval archer detailed to man it. As an important feature in its own right it is particularly well preserved, clearly showing the amount of room available for manoeuvre allowing for multiple angles of fire. Such sophistication is not evident on the only other substantial section of City Wall surviving at St Alphage, an indication perhaps of the special arrangements with regard to defences closer to the Tower of London.

Left out of Cooper's Row is no 43 Trinity Square, a picturesque relic of the Georgian age, originally a bow fronted shop, now the Wine Library. Just to the left of it is an impressive brass plaque of some age headlined *The Roman and Medieval Wall*. 'On this site stands a surviving piece of Roman Wall', it explains, moving on to detail the component parts of the relic and how it was formed. Anecdotal evidence suggests that sometime between the departure of Toc H in the early 1980s and the arrival of the Wine Library in 1988 a much smaller piece of Roman Wall foundation was accessible in the basement. If so then its cellar would have extended as far as the rear of Crescent and with the interior face of the Wall on show. Sadly, enjoying a glass or two of Chateau de la Grille Chinon with a light buffet of pâté and cheese in the company London's ancient Wall is not an option at this city hot spot. Roland Smith, Clerk to the Wakefield & Tetley Trust, confirmed that the newly merged Trust owns (as well as other properties) nos. 41, 42 and 43 Trinity Square and 6, Crescent. Trinity Court, nestling between both properties, was built as part of the 1980s redevelopments, when the remains of the Wall was freed from the adjoining cellar. At the time of writing, huge re-development work is taking place at 40 Trinity Square, where the Museum of London Archaeological Service is carrying out an excavation in the basement to assess the condition of the Wall at that point. Possibly other surviving parts of the Wall might see daylight for the first time in a century or two, to continue on

52 Photograph of the internal face of London Wall, Cooper's Row

53 Photograph of internal face of London Wall towards Tower Hill station

uninterrupted from that already exposed in Cooper's Row. At the time of writing intelligence as to what does or does survive is thin on the ground.

The neighbouring Tower of London underground station opened in 1882 as part of the Metropolitan Railway construction. It was connected two years later to the Metropolitan District Railway (now the District Line) to form the Inner Circle (now the Circle Line). The new station built to accommodate these changes was renamed Mark Lane, and later Tower Hill. These upheavals, the redevelopment work in the 1930s, 1967 and the 1980s have at the same time eroded as much of London's Wall as exposed more of it than at any time in half a millennium. Before 1967 the great length of Wall exposed today on Tower Hill formed part of the London Passenger Transport Building, the rear of which abuts no 6, Crescent.

Elsewhere the remnants of alleyways and buildings recognisable to the antiquaries and chroniclers of old lingered on. John Strype in the early eighteenth century records much of the City Wall between this point and Trinity Square being torn down to create space to build some of these houses. 'The Stones and Rubbish lye there which make a very great Heap', he laments. One part surviving piece of Wall he measured to be about 6 or 7ft feet in breadth. A yard close by called George Alley was lined either side with houses and with a passage leading to Tower Hill knocked through the Wall after the Great Fire of 1666. Probably much like the arch punched through the Wall in Cooper's Row, this passage remained in use for less than fifty years when Strype observed its demolition. '[With] All the Wall quite taken away', he writes, 'one may take a View of the Inside, and of the Breadth of London-Wall: It appears like a natural Rock with the Stones so cemented into the Work, that nothing but the greatest Violence can separate them. On the West-side, about 14 or 15 Foot high are seen several old Roman Bricks put into the Work, between the Stones'. *The Builder* for 4 September 1852 reported on excavations outside of the City Wall on Tower Hill, which uncovered a large number of large wrought and carved stones heaped against the external face of the Wall forming the base of a bastion in a similar fashion to those others uncovered along the Wall. The *Journal of the British Archaeological Association* reported as many as 140 cartloads of stones cut in various forms, evidently belonging to some important building or buildings used to form the base. Mr Fairholt, described as one of the best antiquarian draughtsmen of the day, made an etching of the work in progress showing the extent of the quarry, and adding to the numerous fragments of frescoes with inscriptions, A.H. Burkitt of the Antiquarian Etching Club included one large piece bearing parts of the first three lines of an epitaph set out under a band of laurel leaves. This indicated a monument of considerable magnitude which he duly ascribed it to the memory of a commander of the Roman Navy, but later transpired to be one of the most remarkable archaeological discoveries along the entire length of London Wall.

In 1882, the contractors for the Inner Circle Railway demolished a further 73ft of London's Wall, sweeping away what remained of the southernmost bastion of the group, including its foundation formed of large carved and moulded stones.

54 Photograph of the internal face of London Wall, Tower Hill, 1936

Walter Thornbury, writing later, recalls a substantial length of 'the old fortification' near George Street, which had been incorporated into stables and outhouses. When Walter G. Bell entered Trinity Place almost half a century later a length of that same Wall measuring some 40ft in length, 'but of no great height', was clearly visible displaying alternate courses of stone and Roman tiles and indications that it had been carefully refaced, probably during the fifteenth-century restoration. Another part of its face had disintegrated, however, and so the Society of Antiquaries decided to take the precious fragment under its care, persuading the authorities to repair a canopy fixed to the top of the structure meant to shield it from weather damage. 'This interesting relic of the City Wall will be brought conspicuously under public notice when the Tower Hill Improvement Scheme is carried out, and a clearance made', Bell reported with well-founded optimism. He noted too in the London Passenger Transport Board a 'conspicuous example of a new spirit on the part of a public body to preserve the past.'

    With the London Passenger Transport Board development in 1935, what remained of the last surviving bastion of the group stood four courses high. At its base the builders had placed more large recycled blocks, including one bearing parts of the last line of the same epitaph as that uncovered in 1852. When reunited, it did not commemorate a Roman Naval Commander as previously pronounced, but was erected in memory of Gaius Julius Alpinus Classicianus, 'of the Fabian tribe, procurator of the province of Britain'. The middle lines are missing, but the final part tells that 'his wife Julia Pacata, daughter of Julius Indus, set this up.' The whole piece is thought to have stood over 7ft long and about 5ft high, as the central feature of a large tomb, worthy of such a high ranking official. For this

55 Photograph of the internal face of London Wall , Tower Hill, 2008

was the Roman Provincial Procurator (financial administrator) responsible for the rebuilding of Londinium after Queen Boudicca's burning, an event resulting largely from his predecessor's mismanagement. Part of Classicianus' brief was also to keep a check on the activities of the military governor, Suetonius, to restore the confidence in the Imperial authorities, which was seriously lacking. Due largely to his endeavours, Londinium was developed as a centre for trade and commerce and became increasingly prosperous with villas, temples, a Forum, Basilica and an amphitheatre. Where his tomb originally stood is not known. The surviving fragments of it bear traces of reuse in some other structure before being recycled by the bastion builders. The two substantial fragments from his altar tomb were joined by the third richly carved bolster stone put on display in the British Museum the same year of their discovery, 1935.

In a gesture of goodwill, the London Passenger Transport Board was willing to do what it could to preserve what survived its destruction of London's ancient past. As well as granting every facility for examining and recording the finds in situ, the Board had built a large underground inspection chamber where members of the public (on application for a permit) could see the external face of the Wall showing the plinth stones and two of the masonry and bonding tile courses abutting the northern retaining wall of the railway cutting. 'With thoughtful care for the preservation of the dignity and beauty of the Trinity Place site', writes Walter G. Bell, the Board also faced the western side of their substation with a fine grey stone to harmonise with the exposed City Wall. And built into its wall facing Trinity Square was sunk a carved reproduction of the great inscribed stone slab commemorating Caius Publius Alpinus Classicianus. Steps were also being taken by His Majesty's Office of Works to schedule the surviving length of London Wall above ground as an ancient monument, all of which, Bell remained confident, would in due course provide the precise historic backdrop for the gardens planned to be laid out in front of the underground station by the Borough of Stepney, at the request of the Tower Hill Improvement Council. This was in itself a direct reference to the rich history of the Tower Liberty dividing Tower Hill in two, with that part inside the City Wall known as Great Tower Hill and that outside, in Stepney, Little Tower Hill.

With the Tower Hill Improvement Scheme was realised the enduring monument we see today, as the largest southern most section of London Wall left standing and the last before the Tower. In 1951 Norman Cook agreed with Bell that most of it had been rebuilt, or at least refaced in medieval times, as the scars to its inner face testify. The great gouges revealing the core of double bonding Roman brick were channelled away to create chimney flues for the houses built against it. When opened up in the 1960s, this interior face could be seen for the first time in centuries from the direction of Trinity Square, while the exterior face could just be glimpsed high up on the west side of Tower Hill. Today it is free of all accumulations either side and dominates the gardens as envisaged, providing exactly the backdrop 'Tubby' Clayton pictured.

Complete with its battlements, the original Roman Wall would have been about 20ft high, not far short of the height of the modern walkway. About twice the height again the medieval stonework begins, added when the Wall was repaired and heightened, more irregular and with part of the narrow sentry walk still visible. The memorial to Classicianus is now embedded into a new concrete face replacing the grey stone wall thoughtfully provided by the London Passenger Transport Board. Before it is a sculpted figure, bareheaded and wearing the short tunic of a Roman general with a short sword under his left arm. It stood sentinel in Trinity Place in 1959 before being moved to the gardens in 1968. When construction work began on a new Tower Hill station in 1980, it was moved

56 Illustration of the east face of London Wall and bastion, Tower Hill, from 1819

57 Photograph of the east face of London Wall, Tower Hill. 2008

58 Photograph of Wakefield Park

again to its present position. The plaque on the base explains that the figure is believed to be that of the Roman Emperor Trajan (AD 98–117) and was presented by the Tower Hill Improvement Trust at the request of the Reverend P.B. Clayton. Probably cast in Italy, the late eighteenth-century copy, which may be that of Trajan with the body of Augustus, was found by Dr Clayton in a Southampton scrap metal yard in the 1950s.

Ostensibly the Emperor Trajaw   As part of the improvements in the 1980s, the entrance to Tower Hill underground station was shifted to the present lower level. With the complete liberation of the Wall, so the inspection chamber disappeared, presumably under the walkway. At the time of writing, the construction work going on at 40 Trinity Square continues through to the site of this chamber, offering a rare opportunity to find out what, if anything, of it remains. I wrote, telephoned and emailed all of the obvious agencies but to no avail. Loitering about the scene one day I was approached by a station guard who wondered if I was lost. Two other station officials had previously directed me to the Tower of London. I told him my story. 'Go to the end of platform one,' he replied, 'there's a hatch at the exit end where you can inspect the Wall.' Thanking him profusely I made my way down to platform one, as directed, looking all about me for the observation hatch. Several trains came and went as I searched the length of the platform from end to end. Eventually returning to where I started, by chance I looked up to the ceiling on the other side of the track and there caught sight of a black square above a stone or concrete sill with a tiny lamp playing on the surface. After a few seconds my eyes adjusted to make out the unmistakable face

59 Photograph of London Wall remains, Tower Hill station

of ragstone wall. It measures no more than a metre square and is thickly coated with the black grime emblematic of the London Underground. The ghost of another, much smaller, oblong shaped appendage is visible on the lower part. No doubt it is the shadow of a plaque that once declared something along the lines of 'Portion of the Roman Wall (*in situ*)'.

Some time later, Melissa Humphrys of the London Underground Customer Service Centre came up trumps, capturing the attention of David Divers of the Greater London Archaeology Advisory Service, English Heritage, who confirmed the survival of the chamber. He told me that the Museum of London Archaeological Service will be making a record, the results of which will ultimately be made available through the London Archaeological Archive Research Centre, the Greater London Sites and Monuments Record library and the Tower Hamlets local studies library.

My first hope of exploring the chamber arrived by way of an email from Sir Robert McAlpine Ltd., the construction company employed in the latest transmogrification of Tower Hill. I was invited by Martyn Fawdry, the site supervisor, to tour the site, and a week later found myself face to face with the last phase of ancient inner Wall waiting to shed its skin of modern brick. But it was that lurking on the other side I was aching to see, 'the lost chamber', so tantalisingly close, yet so frustratingly unobtainable. "That's outside of our remit," Martyn explained. "As far as I know," he continued, "only Jane Siddell, the Inspector of Ancient Monuments for English Heritage has been allowed inside there." I hope I hid my disappointment well.

Some of the site archaeologists emerged from their portakabin and told me that they had found traces of a ditch running inside the line of the Wall, which probably pre-dated it. But as to the lost chamber, they were as intrigued as I but were not allowed in. I had met Jane Siddell in a previous life and so thought it worth a begging email to see if she could pull any strings. Sadly it was not to be. Until the nuisance factor finally paid off. Promising to abide by certain conditions, I found myself being guided through a severe monument to inter-war enterprise, down into a dank underworld where there is a black hole in the concrete floor. "You'll need this," said John Reilly from EDF, offering me a torch. "You're not coming down with me?" I enquired gingerly. John had seen it before. Besides, he told me, the place has a certain otherworldly reputation.

At the bottom of the steel ladder leading down into the inky void, I scanned a triangular area measuring less than six square yards. The Roman remains measure three yards long and about five feet high, or six courses of ragstone above the pink sandstone plinth. The first layer of red brick tile banding is clearly visible and like the stone sandwiching it appears to be in good condition, if extremely dirty. A notice of some age is attached to the concrete wall opposite, advising of no works to be effected 'likely to damage or deface Old London Wall in the sub-basement of this building'. This run of much diminished ragstone probably continues deep underground from behind the houses in Crescent and likewise south to reappear in much more dramatic form flanking Wakefield Gardens en route to the Tower of London.

After Wakefield gardens, and at the end of the Tower Hill underpass, are the remains of another substantial London Wall relic. Sitting astride the north bank of the Tower moat, it was clearly built for maximum defence close to the Tower. It's basically a cube highly reminiscent of a Second World War concrete pill box. With an internal length of 11ft, a width of 6ft and walls almost 3ft thick, this is the Tower Postern, the first and last City Gate, and the smallest. Its south wall, straight and featureless, is that facing onto the Tower moat. The east wall representing the entrance into the City is guarded by a pair of arrowslits for archers. Behind the inner most slit is a slot notched in the stone protrusion to accommodate the portcullis. The immense care that went into the defensive design of this structure is evident in every detail, such as the narrow access snaking into the tower behind the portcullis flanked by another arrowslit built into the finger of masonry revealing the settings and iron hinges for a stout wooden gate. This arrowslit also protected the doorway to the guard chamber at the rear where there is evidence of a window and the base of a staircase leading up to a room 11 ft sq with access to the parapet walk. A pointed arch would have joined this tower to the City Wall where there is no evidence to suggest that the same defensive layout was reflected.

John Strype records in the early eighteenth century: 'It sheweth by that Part which yet remaineth, to have been a fair and strong Arched Gate, partly builded of hard Stone of Kent, and partly of Stone brought from Caen in Normandy, since the Conquest, and Foundation of the High Tower, and served for Passengers on Foot out of the East, from thence through the City to Ludgate in the West'. These

60 Photograph of The Lost Chamber

remains were rediscovered in the 1930s under the cellar floor of 19, Tower Hill, one of a number of buildings torn down as part of the plan to create the pedestrianised civic space. Thought to be the oldest postern built into the Wall, in Roman times such a sophisticated defensive point did not exist. There may have been a gate built into the Wall here, or close to this point, but that will never be known for certain, due to the major activity generated by the largest and most continuous construction site in the vicinity over many centuries, the Tower of London.

King Edward I (1272–1307) completed this major defensive work begun by his predecessor, Henry III. Between 1275 and 1285 he had created England's biggest and most powerful castle. The main effort was concentrated on filling in Henry's moat and constructing an additional curtain wall on the western, northern and eastern sides. The replacement moat, however, proved the downfall of the Tower postern, its close proximity gradually undermining its foundations leading to a partial collapse in 1440. As a contemporary account has it: 'the postern be-syde the Towre sanke downe into erthe vii fete'. A replacement gate was resited to the north on the firmer, drier ground, but was a faint echo of its former self, a 'weake and wooden building', more of a 'homely Cottage, with a narrow Passage, made of Timber, Lath and Loam.' Queen Elizabeth granted the tenancy to one Edward Heming, a speculator, who reduced the neighbourhood to the haunt of 'persons of lewde lives'. In rebuilding, Heming fell foul of the Constable of the Tower and the County of Middlesex for enclosing the head of the Town Ditch

61 Photograph of Tower Postern, 2008

and reserving it for the use of his own tenants. The City authorities complained that his actions were devaluing properties and had effectively taken away part of its claim to the land. It might well have been this controversy that brought to a head a centuries' old dispute between the City and the Constable of the Tower as to where the Liberty of the Tower actually lay and the governance of Tower Hill. Sometime over the next century, Heming's rookery became known as Postern Row. Strype records it in the early eighteenth century as 'now all taken down, and in the room thereof a few Posts are set to keep off Carts and Coaches; there being only a narrow Passage left for Foot-passengers there.' George Street, or George Yard, ran between the rear of this warren as far as the southern end of the City Wall revealed today. Built against the Wall and onto this street between 1697 and 1700 were houses, some built by Edward Mount, Stationer to the Navy Office. Much of this development was swept away first by a fire in 1818, and then with the building of the new approach road to Tower Bridge in 1890. Nothing of this ephemeral activity survives today except for the section of City Wall and the Tower Postern in its sunken enclosure.

Before there was a Tower of London there was only the City Wall making its way south to the banks of the River Thames, following the natural contour of the ground governed in part by the streams and lost rivers that have defined the boundaries of settlement in London throughout its history. William the Conqueror built two fortresses to secure his hold on the city, both of which attended the river and each flanked by a protective stream or small river. The 'rough and gloomy' Baynard's Castle was protected to the west by the Fleet. The Tower to the east was protected not only by the Wapping marshes but a hitherto much neglected minor waterway that became 'a great common sewer, or ditch'. It ran to the Thames from the site of a former Roman camp on the London road, later held by the old Soredig, or Soerdich family, lords of the manor in the time of Edward III that afterwards took the name of Shoreditch. An old London legend has it that Shoreditch derives its name from Jane Shore, the enigmatic mistress of Edward IV, who, in 1527, 'worn out with poverty and hunger, died miserably in a ditch in this unsavoury suburb'. In *Percy's Reliques*, Thomas Percy's collection of ballads and popular songs published in 1765, Jane Shore is credited with a passage that appears to combine the 'Sewer-Ditch' with that of Houndsditch:

> Thus weary of my life at length
> I yielded up my vital strength
> Within a ditch of loathsome scent
> Where common dogs did much frequent.
> The which now since my dying daye
> Is Shoreditch called, as authors say;
> Which is a witness of my sinne
> For being concubine to a King.

In his guides out of London via Aldgate and Aldersgate, Strype names Shoreditch church as 'Sewers-ditch-church' and other documentary evidence includes a plan drawn up by Captain I Vetch in 1851, which shows the continuous Shoreditch watercourse running south to the Thames. Vetch's comprehensive scheme produced for the Metropolitan Board of Sewers recommended the requisition of all the 'unobjectionable chalk streams' on either side of the Thames as the future sources of supply of the capital's drinking water and abandoning the Thames altogether, which was increasingly fouled by a population that had doubled within forty years. Without any archaeological evidence we can only imagine 'Sewers-Ditch' taking the same line from the direction of Aldgate to Tower Bridge where it would have exited into the Thames.

Tower Bridge Approach was built in 1907 as the northern access to the £1 million Victorian 'Wonder Bridge'. Before the first of its twin towers is a set of steps leading down to a stone gateway for the outer precincts of the Tower of London and the cobbled road so despised by runners of the London Marathon. Before the Outer Curtain Wall was raised to its current height in the 1330s the Thames covered this whole area as far as the Inner Curtain. After the Devlin and the Well Tower is the Cradle Tower, constructed in 1348–55, and behind that, as part of the older Inner Curtain Wall, is the Lanthorn, or 'Lantern' Tower where a light once burned as a navigational beacon for river traffic when this was the end point of the Roman landward City Wall. At the time of Claudius there was probably a relatively simple timber and stone enclosure nestling beside the Wall 100yds or so behind this last bastion. Towards the end of the Roman occupation a Riverside Wall was built from near enough the site of the Lanthorn Tower to Blackfriars. Before the Norman Conquest most of this wall had collapsed. The compound was later surrounded with a ditch or palisade running in an arc from the river bank to join the Wall. After the Conquest high stone tower was begun around 1078, designed by the celebrated Norman castle builder, Bishop Gundulf, using white limestone from Caen. When it was completed, the solid structure stood 90ft high with walls 15ft thick at the bottom, tapering to 11ft at the top and with the entrance to it above ground level in the Norman fashion. The Normans called it *La Tour Blanche*, or The White Tower. What remained of the Roman Riverside Wall ran as far as the first Water Gate, a tad east of Traitor's Gate. The Roman landward Wall continued to protect the eastern flank, passing by the White Tower to a point at its south-east corner, where a bastion punctuated an oblique angle taking the line of the Wall due south towards the Thames. This arrangement remained unchanged for a century until around 1190 when William Longchamp, Bishop of Ely, Chancellor of England and Constable of the Tower of London, expanded what had become his principal fortress. He extended the Riverside Wall westwards, adding the Bell Tower in the creation of a new Outer Ward. He also included in these works 'a broad and deep Ditch to be made without the same Wall' that was designed to be filled on the tides of the Thames. But despite spending an 'infinite deal of money' on the project however, it didn't work, and served only to add to the Bishop's already faltering reputation. Deeply unpopular with the people and nobility, Prince John returned to England in 1191 to confront his Chancellor, setting siege on the Tower for the first time in its history. As a defensive stronghold it more than proved its worth, but was surrendered by the Bishop after only three days due to a lack of provisions.

Between 1211 and 1213 another huge row erupted, not for the first time, between the Lord Mayor of London and the Lieutenant of the Tower over a proposal to drain the foul contents of the City Ditch directly into the Tower moat, a move permanently tempered some twenty years later when Henry III launched an ambitious building program to make the fortress a royal residence. He had what remained of the Roman Wall demolished to make way for a great new Curtain Wall round the east, north and west sides of the White Tower, doubling the area. Nine new towers were added, the strongest at the corners being the Salt Tower, the Martin and the Devereux. Of these all but the Flint Tower and the Brick Tower are much as originally built. The moat was reworked, possibly by Brother John, a member of the crusading military Order of Saint Thomas of Acre, advised by Master Walter of Flanders, an expert in hydraulic engineering. This was later filled in by Edward I who oversaw construction of an additional Curtain Wall and dug a new moat that would serve the fortress for almost 600 years. It was drained in 1830 after being declared a health hazard by the Duke of Wellington, the then Constable of the Tower, who then had it filled in with rubble and turned into a parade ground as part of the new Wellington Barracks.

Within the Tower, the line of the Roman City Wall is marked out by parallel lines of stone set into the lawn running east of the White Tower to the remains of the Wardrobe Tower where the last fragments of London's Wall survive above ground, happily minus the large green tarpaulin once used to protect these remains from the weather. Built on a Roman bastion, Norman Cook declared the relationship with the Wardrobe Tower to the adjoining stub of Wall better studied here than at any other point. The sandstone plinth continues without interruption through the back of the bastion, clearly indicating a later build and not a part of the original Wall construction. The characteristic triple brick bonding course on the inside of the wall corresponds to the level of the plinth and is offset, thus reducing the thickness of the Wall at this height above its foundation. The bastion was later incorporated into the Wardrobe Tower as part of the improvements made by William Longchamp.

The origin of the modern word wardrobe is derived from Garderobe (the castle toilet), the pungent smells used to deter moths from devouring the expensive gowns. The Wardrobe eventually became a department of the royal household entrusted with the care of personal articles as well as clothing. The Crown Jewels are said to have been placed here in 1244 while work was in progress on Westminster Abbey. In the fourteenth century the king's household developed into the Privy Wardrobe of the Tower, when a large stone building was constructed against the east side of the White Tower to accommodate the administration. As more space was required, so another Wardrobe building was built during the reign of Henry VIII, which was demolished in the seventeenth century leaving the more ancient

62 Photograph of Wardrobe Tower, Tower of London

63 Photograph of foundations of London Wall toward the Lanthorn Tower,
Tower of London, 2008

remains much as they appear now. Sunk into the lawn as far as the Lanthorn Tower are more stones evoking the line of the Roman landward Wall towards its end point at the Thames, and the start of London's riverside defences.

8

The Riverside Wall

Before 1975 perhaps the aspect of Roman London most open to debate was the question of the existence of a defensive Roman Riverside Wall. As well as a reasonable amount of disconnected archaeological evidence before then, there exist only two known documentary sources referring to the mythical structure. The first consists of two land grants dating from the late ninth century referring to an ancient stone building close to the Thames, probably at Queenhithe, citing the 'City Wall' as its southern boundary. The other, and most unambiguous record, is contained in William Fitzstephen's description of London written in 1173, which tells of the City Wall along the Thames eventually cast down by the actions of the tide. Of the three historic occasions when experts think that the Riverside Wall might have been built include the visit of the Emperor Constans in AD 343, the restoration of the defences by General Theodosius in AD 369, or the final Roman expedition organised by Stilico, a high-ranking general of the Western Roman Empire at the very end of the fourth century. Bars of silver and coins from the reign of Honorius (AD 395–410) were found during excavations near the Lanthorn Tower in 1777, indicating the site remained in occupation until the last years of Imperial control.

Throughout the nineteenth century, sections of wall were discovered along the perceived route of the Riverside Wall from the Tower of London towards Blackfriars. Based on these findings the Victoria County History of London in 1909 concluded that all the available evidence, such as it was, indicated that a late Roman defensive fortification probably built to protect Londinium against marauding Saxons did exist. Moreover, Mr. A. W. Clapham, Secretary of the Royal Commission on Historical Monuments, observed in 1928 that the positions of the Lanthorn Tower (although slightly shifted after a modern rebuilding) and those of the Wakefield, the Bell and the Middle Tower northern turret, all stand in the same straight line parallel with the river towards Lower Thames Street. All are spaced the same distance apart similar to the bastions punctuating the landward Wall. The Commission also concluded that the noticeable variations in construction of the pieces of Wall uncovered were due to the unstable character of the river bank or foreshore dependent upon which part the Wall was built. Specifically these include instances of foundations built on rafts of oak piles or a layer of gravel with a footing of ragstone, chalk, and flint set in puddled clay.

More recent excavations at the Tower support the idea that the Riverside Wall was built the same time as the bastions were added to the landward Wall, and that construction was similarly undertaken in individual stages by different gangs of builders on separate stretches. The reuse of architectural material, pink mortar and brick bonding are also indicators of a construction date later than the landward Wall, and contemporary with the eastern sector bastions. In the days of greater debate on this subject, eminent archaeologists such as Sir Mortimer Wheeler, Gordon Home and Frank Cottrill came to the same conclusions. In contrast, Norman Cook, the Keeper of the Guildhall Museum, considered such evidence to be 'rather scanty'. Other distinguished voices, including William Francis Grimes, Ralph Merrifield and Peter Marsden have, at some stage, argued instead for an embankment or quayside rather than a continuous defensive Riverside Wall. This variance of opinion has now mostly abated, but there are still one or two voices expressing the belief that the Riverside Wall is 'a fiction' and others who find it unlikely that the Romans would have left the underbelly of Londinium undefended. There are also the views that such a Riverside Wall lay further south, or that the buildings themselves strung out along the riverside formed a continuous defensible frontage, a not unreasonable suggestion when considering Fauconberg's ill-fated assault on the City from London Bridge in 1471. Then the houses formed a wall and the narrow lanes leading to the water's edge were 'easily stopped with stones'. But in all of this there is the substantial body of evidence found at the Tower of London at the east end and the dramatic discoveries at Baynard's Castle at the west end in the 1970s. With the landward City Wall likened in form to a bow, so the dotted fragments between the Tower and Blackfriars can be joined as straight as its string.

The spacing between the Lanthorn Tower and the Wakefield Tower is about 180ft, the same as that between the Wakefield to the Middle Tower. This same spacing corresponds to that of the Lanthorn and the Wardrobe Tower and probably all the other Roman bastions originally forming the eastern circuit of the landward Wall. In 1955 a massive piece of Wall measuring 136ft was discovered at the Tower of London on the river alignment. It was regarded as medieval, but excavations in 1977–8 proved it to be the late Roman Riverside Wall. Also, evidence found of an earlier Riverside Wall to the west of the junction of the landward and riverside walls quashed the idea that it was a parting gift from the occupiers. The later wall had been built on a chalk raft supported by rows of wooden piles, exactly like the foundations later discovered at Blackfriars, creating a narrow corridor between the two. This may have been a defended approach from the riverfront to a gateway, or a ramp built of dumped material leading from the river to the gate. The wall recorded in the 1950s showed it did extend beyond

64 Photograph of Riverside Wall, Tower of London

the Wakefield Tower and indeed such a continuation was found in 1979 fifteen yards west of the first stretch, its line converging with the inner curtain wall. Excavating a section north of it revealed that it was built on a construction trench that contained what appeared to be timber scaffolding posts, and forty-eight coins dating to the last years of the fourth century were also found. According to Dr Geoffrey Parnell, Keeper of Tower History at the Royal Armouries Museum, has found evidence indicating that the late thirteenth-century Inner Curtain Wall might be built on the line of a pre-existing feature, and also that the position of the White Tower might have been predetermined by a late Roman stronghold.

The only section of Roman Riverside Wall visible above ground is within the Tower precinct, as part of the public display between the Lanthorn and Wakefield Towers. It shows a very different construction to the landward Wall, with all the engineering skill of the Roman army rather than bands of jobbing subcontractors.

The north inner face consists of extraordinarily neat courses mostly of squared ragstone blocks mixed with Purbeck marble, sandstone, chalk, tufa and tile. The south or outer face comprises ragstone with a double course of tiles 3ft 8in from the base with no plinth. The thickness of the wall is about 10.5ft, its core consisting of ragstone mixed with lumps of chalk, tile and opus signinum, alternating with bands of gravely yellow mortar. As well as traces of bracing timbers running through the core, parallel with the north face timber, lacing was found, apparently at the level of the first offset 5ft from the base. The wall did not continue in a straight line but turned to the south at an angle of about 100°, perhaps as the defensive promontory at its junction with the landward Wall. The corner of the angle was built of several large stone blocks from an earlier building, reused to create the required angle. The mortar smeared between the courses was found to be extremely fresh and completely unweathered, due to the bank of soil dumped against it as soon as it was built. Material from this bank included a comprehensive selection of late Roman pottery and over thirty coins, the latest in date being of Valentinian II, AD 389–92 and evidence that this wall was not built earlier than the last years of the fourth century. General Theodosius would have appreciated full well the strategic value of Londinium. Although the city had successfully withstood many a landward attack, he might not have viewed a combined naval assault with quite the same confidence. It's possible he began building the Riverside Wall in about AD 369, with the inner Wall possibly resulting from Stilico's expedition some thirty years later, the last serious attempt by the central authority to retain Britain as part of the Western Roman Empire. Thereafter, the story is one of even more conjecture, based on increasingly less fact.

By the time the Norman White tower was built within the embrace of the eastern stretch of the landward City Wall, its sister fortification fronting the Thames had probably partially collapsed after the site of what is today Traitor's Gate and a ditch was dug to defend the Norman fortress's west and northern flanks from the river. What remained of the Roman Riverside Wall beyond this point probably disappeared as much under the weight of a burgeoning metropolis as to the will of the tides. The line of it today continues beyond the Middle Tower, follows through the Tower shop (formerly the Victorian pump house) and into Lower Thames Street where, at the time of writing, the eye is assaulted by a decrepit post-war eyesore sandwiched between Three Quays Wharf and Sugar Quay.

The Victorian London writer Walter Thornbury recalls workmen finding evidence of the former riverbed in the form of rushes mixed with mussel-shells and the chrysalides of water insects. Also uncovered from this lost foreshore were three distinct lines of wooden embankments spaced apart at 58ft, 86ft and 103ft within the range of the wharves then existing. About 50ft from under the edge of these buildings was also discovered the remains of 'an ancient wall built of chalk and rubble, and faced with Purbeck stone' that ran in an east west direction, or parallel with the Thames. Like its landward counterpart it was so tough that iron wedges driven into it to break it up had little effect. Many coins and other Roman antiquities were found, and rows of oak piles, 28ft and 30ft long sunk into the mud, and onto these beech sleepers fitted in with brickwork. Thornbury had no doubt in his mind that this was part of Fitzstephen's fabled Riverside Wall.

Further along is the vast, extensive, grand and impressive pile that is the Custom House where once a ship's master would register his craft and pay the duty to tie up in the port of London. Measuring 488ft long and 107ft wide, the Long Room is thought to be largest room in Europe. Excavations in 1973 revealed three rectangular Roman posts with sharpened ends that were clearly driven in later that the earlier Roman waterfront. They may have been piles for a wall, although only a few loose chalk blocks survived. The tops of all these timbers were eroded and covered by river gravel which contained worn later Roman pottery. In isolation these finds appear less conclusive than the actual Roman Wall as described by Thornbury, but their position and the character of the piles, the chalk deposits and the fact that they were sealed by river gravels, are all features similarly observed of the Riverside Wall at Baynard's Castle.

The Old Dog Tavern stood on the corner of St Mary at Hill, on the north side of Lower Thames Street, until 1848 when it was torn down to make way for the Coal Exchange, another impressive high Victorian edifice gracing this Thameside thoroughfare. In its heyday it is estimated that 20,000 seamen were employed in the Carrying Department alone. In digging the foundations for the Exchange a Roman hypocaust was discovered, considered to be among the most interesting of all the many Roman remains uncovered during the redevelopment of Victorian London. With tiled floors and several rooms, such was the significance of the find, that part of the complex was preserved and displayed within the basement of the building. Known as the Billingsgate Bath House, due to its close proximity to the famous old fish market, it remains one of the most important preserved sites within the City of London. Further excavation work in 1859 revealed a solid outer wall constructed of Kentish ragstone measuring approximately 7ft thick, its position more towards the old riverfront, its size and lack of association with the bath building suggesting it formed part of the Roman Riverside Wall. Following the Ancient Monuments Act in 1882, the Billingsgate Bath House became one of the first sites to be scheduled in London, and so in 1967 when the Coal Exchange was demolished, the new building on the site was required to allow for the preservation and eventual display of the Roman remains. A programme of monitoring work was carried out by the Museum of London in 1999 during the installation of a new access ramp and entrance. Design changes to the basement area were made to provide for public access to the monument, but, at the time of writing, 101 Lower Thames Street lies empty.

What is known as the 'Billingsgate Buildings Triangle' is today occupied by a shiny pink granite wedge west of Monument Street and Lovat Lane. Archaeological excavations undertaken here in 1974 set out to prove conclusively the existence of the Roman Riverside Wall, centring specifically on a length of masonry found in 1911 about 300ft to the west, where the alignment was spurious and required further clarification. A spread of oak and chestnut piles had been discovered in 'The Triangle' in 1834 closer together and larger in size towards the river. These may have formed part of a quay side structure, although the piled foundations of the Riverside Wall can't be ruled out. In the same year substantial masonry, presumed to be Roman, was discovered further west at the bottom of Fish Street Hill. In 1912, workmen digging foundations opposite on the south side of Lower Thames Street found more remains, which *The Builder* magazine proclaimed unequivocally to be the base of the Riverside Wall. Found 24ft below the street level, resting upon long and thick timber balks laid crosswise, with piles beneath them, onto this base were laid three courses of rough rag and sandstone capped with two courses of yellow bonding tiles, all in reddish mortar, about 3ft high and 10ft wide. The celebrated antiquary Charles Roach Smith had some years earlier recorded the Riverside Wall as having included alternate layers of red and yellow plain and curve-edged tiles, the rest being of ragstone and flint, and founded on piles. The use of red and yellow tiles would probably have been a limited fashion, more likely to be fourth-century.

It is possible that this was the westward continuation of a similar discovery made the previous year while sinking a pier hole for a new building at 125 Lower Thames Street. Here, large, roughly squared timbers were discovered, measuring 12ft in length and about 8in sq, laid on ballast across the thickness of the Wall and held in position by pointed piles driven in at intervals. One of them measured 30in long with a triangular section in the upper part measuring 3×4in by 4.5in. On one of the angles a channel had been cut as if to secure a plank. On these timbers were laid large irregular rag and sandstones bedded in clay and flints. Three layers of these were facing stones, above which was a bond of two rows of yellow tiles. Some chalk, together with other stone formed the core cemented with red mortar. The whole piece measured 3ft high and 10ft wide. Some of the stones were apparently reused, with evidence of shaped or moulded stone. By 1923, William Lethaby also was satisfied that 'full evidence of the course of the City Wall along the river front' had been found.

The 1974 excavation, still looking for that same sense of confirmation, found no trace of the Riverside Wall but what may have been the eastern continuations of the more substantial box-structures excavated on either side of the likely line of the Roman bridge between 1920 and 1929. Work conducted by the Museum of London at New Fresh Wharf, now the site of St Magnus House (no 3, Lower Thames Street), also in 1974, produced a huge collection of Roman artefacts and an imposing timber quay. Although the site stretches from Lower Thames Street to the modern riverbank, only the northern third contained surviving archaeological strata covering three successive periods. As well as second-century river embankment, there was an impressive third-century timber quay running along the back of it, which was probably made redundant by the Riverside City Wall. Dumped material found here included an astonishing array of general household rubbish and numerous examples of imported goods, demonstrating London's prime purpose during the Roman occupation as a port, its business recorded on wooden writing tablets made from cedar, silver fir and Norway spruce. As well as roofing slates from north Wales, there was jet from Whitby and coal from south Wales or Durham and a pilaster capital that may have been imported from northern France. Stone from Kent was unloaded along with Carrara marble from Italy, and the fashions of the day represented the large numbers of leather shoes, jackets and breeches recovered. From about AD 250 the level of the river was dropping in relation to the land and towards the fourth century was silting ports and quays across the southeast of England, including the Thames. The first post-Roman structures discovered on this site were tenth-century rubble banks and stakes laid against the eroded base of the riverside fortification that stymied this bustling centre of trade.

By the time of the Norman Conquest in 1066, a church was standing on this firm ground above the new foreshore and dedicated to St Magnus the Martyr around 1100. One of the petrified timber stumps from the Roman quay rests in the church porch, as does a blackened fragment of Roman Riverside Wall revetment excavated in 1929. St Magnus' was one of the first casualties of the Great Fire, its location being opposite Pudding Lane where the fire started. Another fire destroyed the roof in 1760 and the church suffered bomb damage in both World Wars. A blue plaque links this site to the old London Bridge, several stones of which are also laid out in the churchyard. It stood on the north end of the bridge for some 700 years, probably on the same line as the wooden bridge first established by the Romans. The stone structure built by Peter Colechurch in 1176 and 1209 remained the only bridge over the Thames until Westminster Bridge was built in 1750. It was lined for centuries with shops and houses until as late as 1760 when they were cleared away, along with the City Gates, to ease the flow of traffic. A new bridge started in 1823 by Sir John Rennie was built slightly to the west to minimise disruption and lasted less than 150 years when it was sold to adorn Lake Havasu City, Arizona, in 1972, the buyers believing they had purchased the more ornate Tower Bridge.

Passing under London Bridge, Lower Thames Street gives way to Upper Thames Street where traces of the same quay construction as that found at St Magnus House have been uncovered. In 1863 part of a wall boasting 'Large and interesting specimens of Roman bricks and workmanship' declared some twenty-two years earlier by Roach Smith to be the Roman Riverside Wall, was discovered on the corner of Suffolk Lane with Upper Thames Street. All Hallow's Lane opposite circumnavigates Cannon Street Station via Steelyard Passage, today part of the Thameside Walk. This whole area was once the site of an imposing Roman building complex, originally thought to have been the Governor's Palace, but now believed to have been the seat of central government. The near mythical London Stone, possibly Londinium's *Milliarium Aureum* (Golden Milestone), a common reference point from which all distances were measured, might have originated from this complex, its pitiful remains now displayed behind a grill at 111 Cannon Street. The Steelyard was, in the Middle Ages, the trading base of the Hanseatic League in London. Like other Hansa stations, it consisted of a separate walled community with its own warehouses, weighing house, church, counting house and residential quarters. It survived in various forms despite numerous upheavals of high history until 1853, when the property was sold and Cannon Street Station built on the site shortly thereafter.

The Riverside Wall was interrupted at this point by the outlet of the Walbrook river, considered London's original harbour with numerous quays along its line. Indeed, the stretch of Wall examined by Roach Smith on the east side may have been a quay wall serving this Thames tributary. In Roman times the Walbrook physically bisected the City. Its source in Moorfields took it through the City Wall just west of All Hallows-on-the-Wall towards the site of the Bank of England. About 150ft to the west of the street today named after it was a small valley upon the banks of which the Romans erected their temple to the God Mithras. A still discernible dip survives along Cannon Street between Budge Row and Walbrook. From here the river made its way past the church of St John the Baptist upon Walbrook (demolished to make way for the Metropolitan District Railway), down College Street, formerly Elbow Lane due to the sharp turn it took at this point. Following complaints about its polluted state this lower section was covered over from the middle of the fifteenth century, although the final Dowgate, or river port, section remained open for many years. Today the Walbrook runs some 30ft below the City's streets as the London Bridge sewer, discreetly disgorging its contents into the Thames from an outlet west of Cousin Lane, which leads back from Steelyard Passage to Upper Thames Street.

At the junction with Queen Street in 1839, workmen deepening a sewer in the middle of Upper Thames Street came across a length of Roman Wall at a depth of 10ft, which Roach Smith described as being 'precisely similar in general character,' to his discovery two years earlier. These 'perfect remains of an old Roman wall, running parallel with the line of the river' comprised alternate layers of flint, chalk and flat tiles, which like much of this ancient fortification proved no easy task to demolish. Crossing to Queen Street on the north side, Skinner's Lane passes behind the church of St James Garlickhythe, a name taken partly from the Saxon 'hythe', meaning a landing place or jetty, and where London's most important preservatives, food flavourings and medicines were unloaded and traded. The church may date back to the late Saxon period and was replaced in the fourteenth century. After the Great Fire it was rebuilt by Sir Christopher Wren whose successful introduction of natural light into it lent it the title of 'Wren's Lantern'. St James Garlickhythe escaped major damage during the Second World War, including a 500lb bomb that buried itself in the south-east corner without exploding.

Hereafter the built landscape is challenged. There would be no other reason to enter this looming abyss except to pause opposite Queenhithe and consider Roach Smith's major discovery of 1841 when 'excavations for sewerage commenced at Blackfriars....The workmen having advanced without impediment to the foot of Lambeth Hill were there checked by a wall of extraordinary strength, which formed an angle with the Hill and Thames Street.' It extended, as far as he was able to observe, to Queenhithe with occasional breaks. In thickness the Wall measured from 8–10ft. The height from the bottom of the sewer was about 8ft, with evidence of houses destroyed by the Great Fire seen to 'abut on the wall' at about 5ft. This could indicate to parts of the Roman Wall that were still standing in the seventeenth century being used in the construction of later buildings, or their foundations. To the untrained mind at least, these remains reasonably suggest the existence of a Roman Riverside Wall. Oak piles were first driven into the mud and onto these were laid a stratum of chalk and stones, and then a course of hewn sandstones measuring 3–4ft by 2.5ft firmly cemented into place with a mixture of quick lime, sand and pounded tile. On this substantial 'raft' the Wall was built in the prescribed manner of ragstone and flint with layers of red and yellow, plain and curved-edge tiles. The mortar was equal in strength to the tiles, which 'could not be separated by force.'

Excavations carried out by the Museum of London at the foot of Lambeth Hill revisited a previous investigation for the Guildhall Museum carried out in 1961–62, which identified two periods of massive Roman building. Using nineteenth-century observations of a huge chalk platform, coupled with dendrochronological analysis of the supporting piles, a date was arrived at of AD 294 and the interpretation of a 'palatial administrative complex housing the primary functions of the late Roman state' arrived at. This complex included an armoury, treasury, mint, supply base, offices, residential quarters, temples and public amenities, possibly spawned from part of a massive programme of public works in the south-west area of Londinium's waterfront. Included in this was the Huggin Hill bathhouse, probably a temple and at least one monumental arch or entrance that was subsequently refurbished or rebuilt on more than one occasion prior to construction of the Riverside Wall. Investigations in 2001 and 2003 revealed Roman masonry remains that survived the 1960's construction along the southern part of the Salvation Army Headquarters building, with even more substantial Roman, medieval and post-medieval remains found beneath Booth Lane. The major discovery of a western apse fronting the Thames reflects a previously known semicircular recess to the east, offering substantial clues as to the layout of the Roman buildings here and their functions. The enormity of the later masonry construction extending to the old Sunlight Wharf suggests a massive podium for a temple, measuring around twenty-one metres by eight metres. Covering the later remains were metalled road surfaces, roadside ditches, structural and other occupation activity dating from the eleventh to the seventeenth centuries on the line of Upper Thames Street and Lambeth Hill, but within the Riverside Wall.

The church of St Mary Somerset is first mentioned in the twelfth century and was destroyed in the Great Fire. Rebuilt under the direction of Wren in 1686–95, it was demolished in 1872, leaving only the tower standing. In 1964 archaeologists were allowed a matter of days to excavate an adjoining site which uncovered the remains of a Roman public bath and a section of Roman and post-medieval wall. Beneath the single fragment of architectural interest alongside this minor motorway, is the St Mary Somerset Garden, its few fragrant square yards of clipped box offering a welcome respite as Upper Thames Street gives way to Castle Baynard Street. 'Street' is not an accurate description, for this is more a tunnel, a subway, an underground channel. Apart from the name taken for this burrow, its slight north-westerly rise does echo that of the Roman Riverside Wall at this point, whether deliberately is doubtful, but of some interest none the less. It is as long as it is dank, depressing and repetitive. It passes beneath Peter's Hill and was the capital's first pedestrian river crossing for more than a century straddling the Thames to link the City of London at St Paul's Cathedral with the Tate Modern Gallery at Bankside. Natural daylight creeps in at Benet's Hill, atop of which sits the charming church of St Benet (Paul's Wharf) languishing in splendid isolation as the last vestige of architecture on a human scale. Built by Wren's Master Mason, Thomas Strong, and completed in 1683, it is one of only four churches in the City that escaped damage in the Second World War and as such is especially valuable. The concrete conduit that is Castle Baynard Street continues on, until its desolate, cheerless world gives way to the working face of the Mermaid Theatre and the equally unprepossessing region of Puddle Dock.

In the summer of 1974 massive redevelopment in this area offered an opportunity for the archaeologists to excavate. The most startling discovery was a huge portion of collapsed Roman wall lying on the presumed Roman shoreline. An extended watch was maintained thereafter, and at intervals throughout 1975 and '76 considerably more evidence was uncovered over a total length of some 115m. In varying states of decay, and displaying different methods of construction, these chunks of Roman Wall were similar to the discoveries made all along the ancient Thames shoreline from the Tower of London. Variation of the subsoil made for more or less elaborate foundations. Towards the site of the Mermaid Theatre the subsoil was generally firmer. Further east conditions were less stable. For example a 40m stretch of wall was constructed on a chalk raft supported by tightly packed rows of timber piles dating the construction of the Riverside Wall to the fourth century. The inner face comprised four courses of ragstone set in a rough herringbone pattern, surmounted by a tile course above which was an offset back about 4in. There then followed five courses of ragstone and a double tile course with a much wider offset of over a foot. The same pattern was duplicated above. Flat tiles, or bricks, were employed exactly the same as in the landward Wall, as well as roofing tiles set with the flanges downwards into the mortar, reminiscent of the discovery made by Roach Smith a century earlier. The tile courses did not run the full width of the Wall, the outer face of which had been eroded away by the Thames, just as Fitzstephen had asserted. The core was of rubble concrete formed from ragstone, chalk, flint, tile fragments and lumps of *opus signinum*, again like that at the Tower. Between the second and third tile courses the herringbone work of the internal face gave way to dressed rectangular blocks more reminiscent of the landward Wall. This work was completely covered up by a clay bank against the internal face which survived to a height of over 6ft, possibly as a working platform successively added to as the Wall gained in height. A culvert roughly 8in square and capped by a flat tile was built on a diagonal through the Wall and a corresponding channel created through the clay banked behind.

Further west there was a change in construction. The foundation was no longer piled but instead consisted of large blocks of ragstone rammed into the subsoil, as gravel gave way to clay. Other construction methods shared similarities with the eastern group of bastions added about the same time to the landward Wall, such as the profusion of recycled sculptured stone blocks. Where the Tower Hill bastion gave up the monumental stones of the Roman provincial procurator, Classicianus, so the Blackfriars haul was assigned to a pair of major monuments, one a late second- or early third-century arch richly decorated with figures of classical gods, and the other a screen of Gods carved

65 Photograph of Riverside Wall, Mermaid Theatre, 1975 (1)

66 Photograph of Riverside Wall, Mermaid Theatre, 1975 (2)

on both sides and at one end. The remaining blocks included a relief of four
Mother Goddesses, two altars commemorating the restoration of temples to Isis
and Jupiter and one recording the name of a hitherto unknown Roman governor
of Britain.

During the post-Roman period, the gradually rising level of the Thames not
only caused the ports and quays to silt up, but also to erode the southern face
of the Riverside Wall in places to about half its original width. But while this
evidence supports Fitzstephen's claim that the Wall eventually succumbed to the
action of the Thames, a part at this western end was found to have collapsed
inwards, away from the river, offering the suggestion that it was deliberately
demolished. Given the incredible importance of the Thames to this great trading
city, it would have been inconceivable to retain such an effective barrier. Huge
efforts must have been made over a long period of time to break it down for the
establishment of new ports and quays. Yet there is no evidence or record of such
a systematic demolition. By the middle of the twelfth century a gravel foreshore
had formed against the surviving masonry, dating the demolition sometime
before the construction of the timber waterfront to the first half of the thirteenth
century. William Fitzstephen's description of Norman London was drawn
together sometime before 1183, suggesting that he must have been familiar with
surviving sections of the Riverside Wall in his own lifetime, as much as he was
its landward counterpart. Apart from private charters relating to land transactions
in the City, we have no detailed account at all of what Norman London actually
looked like. There is no description in the Domesday Book. What is now certain
is that part of the Roman Riverside Wall was extant in Fitzstephen's day as part
of the 'Palatine Citadel', or what would become the Tower of London. To the
west the 'two strongly fortified Castles' of Baynard and Montfichet sat beside the
landward Wall running continuously along the line of the River Fleet south to
the Thames.

The first of the three castles to bear the name of Baynard in this quarter was
built north of Queen Victoria Street by Bairnardus, or Baynard, a Norman who
accompanied William the Conqueror in 1066. Immediately north of it, towards
modern day Ludgate Hill was Montfichet's Tower. Together these 'two most strong
castles…built with Walls and Ramparts' sat within the Roman Wall running
parallel with the River Fleet towards the Thames. In the year 1111, William
Baynard succeeded to and lost these properties as a result of a felony, with Robert
FitzRichard granted the honour. Having overcome the small matter of rebellion
in 1215, the then incumbent, Robert Fitzwalter, was granted a licence by Edward I
in 1275 to convey both castles to the Archbishop of Canterbury for the foundation
of a House and Church for the Dominican Order of the Black Friars. In 1282 the
City Wall was broken down from Ludgate to the Thames. A quay was built and the
priory lands were extended to the River Fleet and Puddle Dock. Baynard's Castle
was rebuilt in 1317, when surviving remnants of the Riverside Wall were used as
the foundation for the north wall. A great fire in 1428 destroyed that version and
Humphrey, Duke of Gloucester, 'builded it new' further to the east, about where

the Mermaid Theatre stands today. On his death in 1446 it came into the hands of Henry VI and then Richard, Duke of York, who lodged there 'as his own house' in 1457. Sir Thomas More records that on the death of their father, the infant sons of Edward IV, Edward and Richard, were 'practised here for Crown,' by Richard Duke of Gloucester, then Protector, who took on the 'Title of the Realm, as offered and imposed upon him, in this Baynard's Castle'. Edward and Richard are perhaps best remembered as the ill-fated princes in the other Tower at the east end of the Riverside Wall. In 1487, Henry VII rebuilt Baynard's Castle not as a strongly fortified castle but as something 'far more beautiful and commodious for the Entertainment of any Prince or great Estate.' Here he lodged with his queen on many occasions throughout his twenty-four year reign, worshiping at St Paul's Church and entertaining foreign dignitaries. In 1505 he, together with the Knights of the Order, 'all in their Habits of the Garter', rode the streets of the City from the Tower of London to the Cathedral Church of St Paul's and then to Baynard's Castle. The next day they rode again in procession to St Paul's. It was demolished that same year to make way for residence more befitting great state occasions and more famously as the residence of the Earls of Pembroke. The Earls of Shrewsbury were the last to occupy the famous castle when it fell victim to the Great Fire of 1666. Today the name Baynard lives on as a City Ward, a lacklustre office block and the grimmest thoroughfare in the City of London.

Postscript

It is often stated that no period in the history of Britain is as mysterious as that between AD 450 and 600. London is believed to have been deserted in favour of a new settlement further west towards the Strand. If so, the questions arise, when was all the built Roman infrastructure dismantled, by whom and using what means? There must have been entrepreneurs prepared to keep the engine ticking over even if most of the passengers had deserted the ship. In his book *Londinium: London in the Roman Empire*, John Morris explains in great detail post-Roman London's role as the principal link between Britain and Europe, the old world and the new. Although the archaeological evidence is slight, Morris cites the 'stout barrier' of the City Wall making London 'the pivot of political and military contention'. Indeed, there does appear to be sufficient historical record before the Dark Ages to show that London held out as the Roman Empire declined and the new invaders made inroads. London was a fortress beyond the reach of an enemy unable and ill-equipped to undertake a siege on the scale required to overwhelm it. If any occupier was to hold out anywhere in Britain, then it was London. The Romans had strengthened its defences landward and riverside, and the result would have resisted natural and piecemeal human erosion for centuries. Throughout all of the turbulent times leading up to the Norman invasion, London's influence governed by its place in the emerging world and its ability to defend itself, must have remained a constant.

Ralph Merrifield, on the other hand, makes the case that London without its trade and industry or government service can only have supported a tiny population eking a living from the Thames and neighbouring fields close to the City Walls. The standing garrison required to maintain 'a minimal 24-hour watch' of the Walls and its gates he estimated to be around 1000; 'an impossible number of mouths to be fed from a local subsistence economy'. Moreover, in the absence of an organised state able to spread the burden more widely by some form of taxation, London would have had no access to an adequate garrison in times of great emergency. Under these circumstances, it is argued, life inside the Wall could be more dangerous than in the open countryside, where there was a better chance of escape from a surprise attack. The possibility of a small fortified citadel, perhaps on the site of the Tower of London, acting as a refuge is not discounted. But then would it necessarily have been any safer, and did London require such a large garrison on constant watch? Let us imagine say, ten men per bastion alternating on a two-man watch around the clock. That's 200 men. The same number of men manning the seven gates, that's another seventy, making a total permanent standing watch of less than 300. These men could have been mercenaries hired by what was passing for the City Fathers. Soldiers of fortune would have come and gone over time, with London a far more attractive proposition than earning a living outside the Walls. Also, its reputation would have retained sufficient currency to deter any notion of the scale of combined land and river attack required to take it.

The lack of Saxon and other mid-term archaeology in London also suggests an absence of post-Roman occupation. Perhaps the later occupiers utilised what they found and without any building programme requiring a lot of digging, what was lost was minimal. Except for ritual or religious reasons, which can be dubious at the best of times, why go to all the effort of demolishing perfectly good and immensely strong buildings to replace them with wattle and daub? Possibly the marks they did leave were eradicated by the Normans and their building programme. London was nothing like other isolated Roman settlements, vulnerable and open to attack from a constant stream of incomers. It was the finest fortified town in the land and so people would have stayed and adapted their surroundings to their needs over time. No different from any other medieval fortification, those living and working in the forests and fields outside would have sought shelter inside the City Walls in time of danger and assisted in keeping attackers out.

It is highly unlikely that nature and the subsequent occupiers eradicated all or most of Roman London by the time William Fitzstephen came to put quill to parchment. Written as an introduction to the Life of Thomas Becket, Fitzstephen's observations are widely regarded as a vivid account of the topography, population and monuments of the City of London in the twelfth century. If fact, his observations are really quite limited. He makes no mention of the original site of the Guildhall, which takes its name from the Old English *ealdormanna burh*, or fortified enclosure of the Aldermen. It is believed that the leading citizens of the City required some protection for their place of work, which is contained in that Old English name. Could not the name of that fortified enclosure refer to its location within the boundary of the Roman Cripplegate fort, or Aldermanbury?

Within the context of the Riverside Wall, Fitzstephen writes as though in his day it was all gone, thus fuelling centuries of doubt and debate. Of London's Wall he writes: '…there runs continuously a great wall, high with seven double gates, and with towers along the north at intervals. On the south, London was once walled and towered in like fashion, but the Thames, that mighty river, teeming with fish, which runs on that side with the sea's ebb and flow, has in course of time washed away those bulwarks, undermined and cast them down'. In this he offers no more evidence for the existence of the landward Wall than he does its riverside counterpart, yet these few words have served to fuel a controversy spanning 800 years. The only surviving architectural remains of Norman London today are the White Tower, the crypt of St Mary-Le-Bow, the choir of St Bartholomew's church, part of the Temple church and the crypt of St John of Jerusalem. But then London has undergone more transformations than any other British city since 1066, far more in terms of development and redevelopment than the 600 years after the Romans left and the Normans arrived. Developers throughout the nineteenth and twentieth centuries used everything from dynamite to mechanical diggers to demolish bits of the Roman Wall. So what of the great Roman Basilica and forum, the largest building north of the Alps? It cannot have completely gone by the eleventh century – likewise the amphitheatre, the temples and the baths. Much of the area around Cannon Street Station was the Roman equivalent of Whitehall, which long after Fitzstephen's time, became the separate walled community of the Hanseatic League in London and must have incorporated parts of the imposing Roman remains in its warehouses, weighing house, church, counting house and residential quarters. The theory that an imperial treasury was kept in Londinium provides one reason for the building of a fortified Riverside Wall, which if true would have been far better sited here at the seat of central government, beside the main quay. Essentially there has been more theory than fact in all of this.

Today it is entirely possible to walk much of London Wall without deviation, but it is not a practical proposition. Permissions and restrictions notwithstanding, London has outgrown its Wall, long since discarded it like an old jacket. Its removal has been a process that has gone on quietly and steadily over many centuries. The buildings of the last two centuries have plunged far deeper than before into the fabric of London's past, eradicating its history, much of it unrecorded. Nature and neglect have played their part in its loss over time, as much as theft and wilful damage. As late as 1937, the continued concern of the Sovereign for the safety of the City was still expressed at the beginning of each quarter of the year. The Secretary of State for War passed to the Lord Mayor, via the Governor of the Tower of London, a set of passwords to the Gates of the City of London, one password for each day of the ensuing three months. When Walter G. Bell reported this tradition, 160 years had passed since the last City Gate disappeared. 'We have seen how little of the Wall is left,' he writes. 'Yet its 'Ghost' is a substantial one – for the Order making the passwords is signed by the King himself.' When that transmission from monarch to mayor ceased is not clear. Neither the Lord Mayor's Office nor the Tower has any knowledge of it today. More of the Wall is now visible since those orders were issued. That it is so, and that we enjoy far more access to it, is down almost entirely to a curious combination of enemy bombs and otherwise reviled post-war planners prepared to slot the old into their brave new world.

Appendix I

Walking London Wall
Field Guide

Preparation

There are some points on the route that require pre-planning in the form of booking an appointment, or at least making sure that the venue is open. For security reasons, it is not possible to see the remains under the Central Criminal Court. Entry to 31 Jewry Street and 35 Vine Street is strictly by appointment only. The Departure Bar in Crutched Friars is open to paying customers only. The following details of these and other buildings and open spaces are correct at the time of writing.

Amen Court belongs to the Chapter of St Paul's Cathedral and permission is required to enter it. Contact the Secretary to the Clerk of Works on 020 7236 4128.

The Viaduct Tavern is open from 11am-11pm on weekdays only. The old Newgate cells can be viewed by appointment: 020 7606 8476.

Merrill Lynch Headquarters: Call the security desk on 020 7996 9777 or 020 7995 9766. Public viewing is between 9am-5pm Monday-Friday and 9am and 1pm Saturday. Sundays and other statutory holidays are excluded.

Roman Fort, London Wall: Tours of 30 minutes' duration are undertaken by the Museum of London. Assemble in the Museum foyer at 11am or 12pm usually on a Monday, Tuesday or a Wednesday, sometimes on a Sunday. There's no need to book. For confirmation of the days and times, visit the Museum website: www. museumoflondon.org.uk. Note: this is an 'Adult Event', subject to a minimum age eighteen requirement.

All the **parks, gardens and open spaces** on the route are subject to opening times, usually daylight hours, weekdays throughout the year, and on weekends between 1 April and 30 September, except for during the Christmas and New Year period.

All Hallows-on-the-Wall is open to the public most Fridays from 11am-3pm. Please call first to check: 020 7588 8919.

31 Jewry Street: strictly by appointment only. Write to the Workplace Support Supervisor, London Metropolitan University, 31 Jewry Street, London EC3N 2EY

35 Vine Street: write to: Field Fisher Waterhouse LLP, 35 Vine Street, London EC3N 2AA. Visits strictly by appointment only.

The Tower of London: If you want to include a visit to the Tower as part of this walk, then it is advisable to purchase tickets in advance. Visit www.hrp.org.uk/toweroflondon for details.

101 Lower Thames Street: Tour details and charges of the private baths used to be part of the Museum of London Events, but this is not clear at the time of writing.

The Walk

The rigours of negotiating the City of London depend on when and what time you decide to travel. A weekday between 8am and 9am will allow you to take part in the full stampede of City workers, whereas after 10am you will be able to set your own pace. Weekends offer a different world altogether with Square Mile mostly given over to tourists. Then, however, you miss out on the essential vibrancy of the place, and possibly access to some of the route. Dispel any notion of driving into the City of London, or even cycling the route. This is a walking exercise pure and simple. London is made up of Travel Zones that determine how much you pay to travel on buses, tube and underground trains, the more zones you cover. Blackfriars station is a London Underground and National Rail station in Travelzone 1. Both are located immediately east of Blackfriars Bridge at the junction of New Bridge Street and Queen Victoria Street. The National Rail station has both through and terminal platforms covering services from Bedford and Luton in the north and Brighton in the south via London Bridge. There is also a peak-hour service that includes Gatwick airport. The London Underground station is on the Circle and the District lines. The London River Services run from Blackfriar's Pier, adjacent to Blackfriars Bridge. However, no sooner are these words writ than the three-year closure of Blackfriars Underground Station is announced from March 2009. Temple and Mansion House Underground stations are each about a quarter of a mile from Blackfriars station, but for the purposes of this exercise Temple Station is recommended. So, if you are following these directions before the closure of Blackfriars underground station, turn right on leaving the ticket barrier and out into the dubious delights of Queen Victoria Street, and then right (east) for Puddle Dock. Post March 2009, turn left out of Temple Station onto the Victoria Embankment. On reaching Blackfriars Bridge take the underpass to Queen Victoria Street and Puddle Dock.

Between no 1 Puddle Dock and Blackfriars Passage lies underground the western tip of the Roman Wall where it met the shoreline of the Thames around AD 200. Looking back from the river towards Queen Victoria Street is the pink striped Bank of New York Mellon Centre and its glass atrium representing the line of the Wall heading north. Cross Queen Victoria Street, using the pedestrian crossing, and turn right for St Andrew's Hill and its Shakespearean connections, particularly the Cockpit Inn with its medieval cellars. Ireland Yard is to the left, once a gateway into the thirteenth Black Friars Monastery. Church Entry, the third turning on the right, is part of the churchyard of St Anne Blackfriars, where a fragment of medieval rubble wall is exposed. In one of the offices close by is a fourteenth-century medieval window protected by a sheet of plate glass, but this is not accessible to the public.

Ireland Yard gives way to Playhouse Yard, the site of the Priory's upper frater, or refectory, where Parliament met in the fourteenth century, the State Record Office was maintained, and a court sat to hear Henry VIII's divorce case against Catherine of Aragon. The unusual width of Playhouse Yard provides a turning circle for carriages when this was once the site of the Blackfriars Playhouse. In the eleventh century this was the site of Baynard's Castle, built shortly after the Norman Conquest. Euromoney House, the former Georgian townhouse facing into Playhouse Yard, has a tower-like corner to the rear possibly echoing the castle's south west turret.

Turning right out of Playhouse Yard there is the hall belonging to the Worshipful Society of Apothecaries. Its seventeenth-century interior dates from the reconstruction following the Great Fire of 1666 and the external appearance has altered little since the late eighteenth century. Continuing north, Blackfriars Lane meets Ludgate Broadway and Carter Lane. Carter Court, a few feet east of this junction, follows the line of the original Roman Wall and is believed to be the only built structure surviving from the Great Fire between the Monument and Temple. Carter Lane represents the southern boundary of Montfichet's Tower, first recorded in 1136. Ludgate Broadway gives way to Pilgrim Street, which leads out to Ludgate Hill with St Paul's Cathedral to the right and Ludgate Circus to the left, with Fleet Street beyond. Directly opposite is the Wren church of St Martin-within-Ludgate, and next to it Ye Olde London public house. The church represents the first building inside the City Wall and the pub where the original north end of Lud Gate once stood. Walking down Ludgate Hill and stepping briefly out of London's ancient City limit, the road can be crossed at a central reservation. Turning back up the hill passes Old Bailey, named after the early defensive outwork (or bailey) cut outside the City Wall, but now more

familiar as the colloquial name of the Central Criminal Court, which lies to the
to the north.

In 1760, the year of George III's accession, all of London's City Gates were
seen as an impediment to traffic, and therefore trade, and were taken down.
The beer garden deep in the bowels of Ye Olde London sits directly on the
line of London Wall. Many Roman and thirteenth-century remains have been
uncovered hereabouts over the centuries, including the substantial remains of
a bastion, or tower, containing Roman artefacts and the City Ditch measuring
22ft from top to bottom. The church of St Martin-within-Ludgate originally sat
as the first and last building on the City limit at this point. It was destroyed in
the Great Fire and not rebuilt until 1703, when it was set back from its old site
with the widening of Ludgate Hill. Major rebuilding and alteration took place
in 1894, but it received the least amount of damage of all the City churches in
the Second World War.

Moving up Ludgate Hill in the direction of St Paul's Cathedral, Stationer's
Court is a slim passage on the left. It was chosen by the Stationers Company for
the site of their Livery Hall in 1611. During modernisation in the early 1800s, an
inscribed Roman memorial was discovered, as well as the remains of the Roman
and Medieval City Wall and gateway. The more contemporary gate immediately
to the left on entering the Court offers a glimpse of a high brick wall to the
rear of St Martin's church and Ye Olde London's beer garden, which sits on the
foundations of Roman London Wall. On the far side of Stationer's Court there
is a small passage leading out into Amen Corner, and on the left is Amen Court
where this same wall continues. Permission is required from the Chapter of St
Paul's Cathedral to enter Amen Court, a rare residential quarter containing late
seventeenth-century houses built for the Canons of St Paul's. This massively high
wall sitting on its Roman foundations once shielded the passageway walked
by condemned prisoners to their executions, who were then buried beneath
it. Known as 'Dead Man's Walk', the passageway survives on the other side and
is a grisly favourite of City ghost tours. If permission hasn't been obtained to
enter the Court then left out of Amen Corner into Warwick Lane and the highly
ornate red brick building that is the entrance to Amen Court, where a good view
of this grim relic can be obtained.

Next left is Warwick Square. In the far left-hand corner is Warwick Passage
and at its mouth a tiny open space featuring a stone pillared arbour, from where
the high brick wall in Amen Court can be seen joining the 1970s extension to
the Central Criminal Court. The line of the City Wall continues under Warwick
Passage towards a large chunk of Roman Wall in the courthouse basement, which
is not on view to the public.

Emerging from Warwick Passage into Old Bailey is to leave the precinct of
the City of London and walk the line of the City Ditch past the famous façade
of the Central Criminal Court, designed by E. W. Mountford. Crossing Newgate
Street at the traffic lights is the Viaduct Tavern, opened in 1869, the same year as
Holborn Viaduct to the left, the world's first flyover connecting Holborn with

Newgate Street. The cellars of the Viaduct Tavern are former cells of Newgate prison and tours may be arranged by appointment.

On the northern face of the Central Criminal Court building is a blue plaque recording the last of the City Gates to be demolished in 1777, Newgate. Believed to have been the principal Roman western gate first constructed in about AD 200, it was rebuilt in the twelfth century to ease the traffic congestion from Aldgate in the east. This New Gate also doubled as a gaol, eventually becoming the most notorious prison in British history. Completely destroyed in the Great Fire, it was rebuilt much stronger and more appropriate for the purpose, and was eventually replaced by the even more notorious gaol that took its name, which was demolished in 1907 to make way for the Central Criminal Court.

To pick up the line of the City Wall, take the alleyway beside no 115 Newgate Street, which leads into the Merrill Lynch Financial Centre and turn left. Just before the exit onto Giltspur Street there is a bronze plaque on the wall and textured paving marking the line of the City Wall. A section of Wall and bastion survive underground and arrangements have to be made in advance to visit these remains. To follow the line of the Wall, turn right onto Giltspur Street as far as Security Gate 1 at the northwest corner of the Merrill Lynch building. The remains are 20ft below in an underground chamber. Here the London Wall turns at a 30 degree angle north-east, following the line of the service road running to King Edward Street. This is a private road, however, with no public access. Returning to Newgate Street and the churchyard of Christ Church Greyfriars, turn left before the vestry for thirteenth-century Christian Passage leading onto King Edward Street. The father of the Post Office, Rowland Hill, stands fittingly before the grand façade of the former General Post Office building, which ends at the mouth of the Merrill Lynch service road and picks up the line of London Wall.

The venerable red brick gateway on the opposite side of the street is the entrance to Postman's Park, famous for its unique memorial celebrating selfless nineteenth-century Londoners who sacrificed their lives to save those of others. On entering the park, the line of buildings to the right represents the exterior face of London Wall and the park itself, the City Ditch. The picturesque red-brick church at the eastern exit of the park is that of St Botolph-without-Aldersgate, which stands by the road that also takes its name from one of the oldest City Gates, Aldersgate.

Aldersgate Street was designated in the 1920s the A1 trunk route, the longest numbered road in the United Kingdom at 409 miles long connecting London with Edinburgh. A blue plaque on the wall of the Lord Raglan public house marks the site of the City Gate, Roman in origin and variously 'beautified' and rebuilt over the centuries with a central arch for general traffic, and two arches either side for pedestrians. Like all the other City Gates, Aldersgate was demolished in the eighteenth century to facilitate the explosion of trade pouring through the City. The line of the City Wall is retained in walls of Lord Raglan's cellars, although all the original stones have long since gone. The first turning on the left moving south from The Lord Raglan is Gresham Street and the church of St Anne & St Agnes, first mentioned in 1467 as St Anne and St Agnes-within-Aldersgate. Left again is Noble Street exposing 1900 years of London history from the Romans to the Blitz.

Most of west Noble Street comprises a huge trench containing the remains of the Roman fort's west wall, including the foundation of an internal turret and evidence of how it was incorporated into the City defences around AD 200. Substantial sections of the medieval Wall survive with nineteenth-century brickwork as far as the 1960s City thoroughfare that takes the name London Wall. Immediately beneath it at this point are the remains of the Roman fort's west gate. If joining a Museum of London tour, then turn left for the escalator (or lift) to the raised walkway leading to the Museum and the foyer assembly point. If not, then cross London Wall using the central reservations. To reach the bastion below and its component parts of City Wall, turn right and take the access road leading down to 140 London Wall and the underground car park. There is no pavement or sidewalk so care needs to be taken with regard to traffic.

There are two ways to proceed, either on the grassed area, or the paved footpath bounding 140 London Wall. The latter takes in the remains of three bastions and surviving parts of London Wall as far as the water feature evocative of the ancient City Ditch, and the former a 'behind the scenes' experience. There are some steps onto the grass at the mouth of the bastion, which lead to the foundations of the second bastion and the herb garden planted therein. There is also a narrow path between a surviving piece of Wall and Barber-Surgeon's Hall.

The bastion dipping its toe into the water at the far end represents the northwest corner of the Roman fort, which extends east to include parts of the north wall. However, this is a residential area, with no entry to non-residents. For the best view of the north wall remains, return to the access road on London Wall and take the steps leading down to Monkwell Square and Barber-Surgeon's Hall. At the northeast corner of the square is a road leading into Wood Street. Turn left towards the north end of Wood Street and left again into St Giles' Terrace, where the medieval church of St Giles' Cripplegate sits incongruously at the heart of the thrusting Barbican Estate. The remains of another bastion can be seen across the water and a section of Wall.

Returning to Wood Street, Fore Street runs off to the left, where the first bomb landed on the City of London in 1940. Ahead is St Alphage, a narrow road to the left. Here on the wall of Roman House are two plaques marking and explaining that this is the site of Cripplegate, the original Roman fort's north gate, built around AD 120. St Alphage Gardens contains a huge section of London Wall. A church here was dedicated to St Alphage in the eleventh century, utilising the City Wall as its northern boundary. By 1872 the former churchyard had become a small public garden. The church was pulled down in 1923 after air-raid damage in 1916. The entrance gate also provides access to Salters' Garden opened in 1995 to commemorate the 600th anniversary of the Worshipful Company of Salters, which has the old City Wall as its southern boundary. Exiting by the same gate and continuing east along St Alphage are the remains of the fourteenth-century church tower to the right. To the left is a covered passage leading to Fore Street, where turning left leads to the entrance to Salters' Hall for a panoramic view of the external face of the Wall, and turning right follows the line of London Wall towards Moorgate.

Moorgate is the only City Gate to have taken its name from the landscape. A blue plaque behind the concrete leg supporting 84 Moorgate marks the site of the Gate, which first appeared as a small pedestrian gate in the Middle Ages, when the wide-expanse of swampy marsh called Moor Fields was being tamed. By 1672 the gate had become an imposing ceremonial entrance, but lasted only a century before it was demolished and its stones used to support the newly widened centre arch of London Bridge.

After Moorgate, the line of London Wall continues in name past the site of Bethlem Hospital, or Bedlam, as it was more commonly known, founded for lunatics and where people flocked to see the patients chained in cells in galleries. Finsbury Circus represents its eastern limit. Drainage of the fens here began after the Romans left, when the culverts cut into the City Wall were blocked to allow for the flow of the Walbrook river. Early in the fifteenth century, the level of the moor had been raised and laid out with elm trees and benches, the area becoming London's first public park. A long stretch of City Wall was demolished in 1817, when the Circus began to take shape as the fashionable medical quarter of London.

After Blomfield Street, the City Wall emerges from below ground in the form a brick wall belonging to the church of All Hallows-on-the-Wall, first mentioned in 1120 and particularly celebrated in the Middle Ages for its hermits. The cell was created from the Roman bastion added to the Wall for extra protection in the late third century AD, shortly before the Roman armies were recalled to defend Rome. Today the vestry sits on the bastion foundations, although viewing is not possible. The brick wall, however, eventually gives way to medieval stone, also sitting on extensive Roman foundations.

After Old Broad Street, the line of London Wall is preserved by the rear of the properties lining Wormwood Street, which originated as a row of small buildings erected against the City Wall in the late seventeenth century. The remains of another bastion were uncovered during redevelopment. Wormwood Street gives way to one of the most important roads in Roman Britain, Ermine Street, which ran from London north to York (Eburacum) and beyond. Today it takes the name of another ancient City Gate, Bishopsgate, the name drawn either from Erkenwald, the son of King Offa, or its access to the vast lands belonging to the Bishopric, now Tower Hamlets. As well as providing accommodation for hermits, and used to display the heads of criminals as a warning to any potential miscreant entering the City, Bishopsgate was rebuilt in 1479 as London expanded east. In common with all the other City Gates it was torn down in 1760. All that remains, at the time of writing, is the cast of a Bishop's Mitre on the upper wall of Boot's the Chemist on the corner of Wormwood Street and Bishopsgate, marking the site of the gate.

Camomile Street, opposite Wormwood Street, is named after the fragrant herb, allegedly grown to counter the stench of the City Ditch. The remains of other bastions have been found between here and Houndsditch described of Roman construction. Also uncovered was 'the Camomile Solider' the earliest known depiction of a Londoner in the form of a tombstone statue.

Camomile Street merges into Bevis Marks where the line of the Wall shifts to the south side of the street. The small courtyard off nos. 10–12 Bevis Marks contains Britain's oldest synagogue. Bevis Marks gives way to Duke's Place, where the subway cut through the line of the City Wall includes a mosaic mural showing the construction of the Roman Wall and the various ground levels since. Take Exit 1 in St James' Passage (before the rear of the Sir John Cass's Foundation C of E Primary School), the mural is to the left directly under the road. Take Exit 6 for the end of Duke's Place and Aldgate, the site of the last City Gate before the Tower of London.

The Museum of London plaque on the school playground wall indicates what the Roman gate may have looked like, built here when the City Wall was constructed. The gate was rebuilt between 1108 and 1147. The poet Geoffrey Chaucer lived in rooms over the gate where he started *Canterbury Tales*. The gate was rebuilt again in 1606 to improve the traffic flow, and demolished altogether in 1760 for the same reasons. On the other side of Aldgate the line of London Wall continues under the east side of Jewry Street. Number 31 was erected in 1899 to the design of A. W. Cooksey, and extended in 1934 for the Sir John Cass Foundation and is now part of the London Metropolitan University. Fragments of London Wall preserved in the basement can be viewed by appointment only.

Entering Crutched Friars from Jewry Street, Roman Wall House is a few yards on the left. Here the Departure Bar has a substantial chunk of very well preserved Wall in its basement, but there is no public access to the remains. Another piece of Wall can be viewed from the other side of the block. At the bottom of Crutched Friars turn left into Crosswall, and then left again for Vine Street and no 35 (Emperor House), the offices of Field Fisher Waterhouse. The remains are preserved under glass at the rear of the building, but prior permission is required to enter the property.

Returning to Crosswall and into America Square, fragments of the City Wall and its associated bastions lie below the surface, or were destroyed during the building of the railway. After the railway arch is Crescent where what remains of the 1930s utilitarian Passenger Transport Board building abuts no 6. Number 7 was the home of the Revd 'Tubby' Clayton until he died. Returning to the railway arch, the passage immediately to the left leads to the largest and best preserved section of London Wall, surviving to a height of 35ft. The lower 14ft is Roman and stands to the height of the sentry walk. During the medieval period it was heightened by 21ft with irregular masonry, and with loopholes which could be used by archers.

Turning left into Cooper's Row and Trinity Square, note the brass plaque on the wall to the left of the Wine Library, the blue plaque dedicated to the memory of 'Tubby' Clayton, and on the wall of no 41, the dedication to Lord Wakefield.

A small section of London Wall is on display in Tower Hill underground station at the end of Platform 1. Above ground is another 100ft length of London Wall standing to a height of 35ft. Stones recovered from the foundations of the fourth-century tower (now gone) included part of the memorial inscription from the tomb of Julius Classicianus, the Roman Provincial Procurator in AD 61, a copy of which is in the park below, facing the bronze statue of the Emperor Trajan.

The Tower Hill underpass leads to the medieval postern gate, uncovered during excavations in 1979. The Tower of London moat beside it was dug in the 1270s, and the gate was probably built soon afterwards, perhaps replacing an earlier structure. It was smaller than the main City gates, intended for pedestrian access only. Looking towards the Tower from this point is to imagine the City Wall in Roman times extending due south to the River Thames. To follow the line of the Wall, turn left into Tower Gardens and then up to Tower Bridge Approach. Just before the first bridge tower, take the steps down to what would have been the Thames foreshore less than 1000 years ago. After the café is the Cradle Tower, constructed in 1348–55 and behind that, a little to the left, is the Lanthorn, or 'Lantern', Tower marking the end point of the landward City Wall.

Ticket holders for the Tower of London should follow the signs for the Crown Jewels. At the east end of the Jewell House, in the direction of the shop, face the White Tower to see two parallel lines of stone sunk into the lawn. These represent the line of London Wall towards the ruins of the Wardrobe Tower. Here the last fragments of the landward Wall survive above ground with the Wardrobe Tower itself built on the remains of a Roman bastion. It was later incorporated into the improvements made by William Longchamp, and later still developed into the Privy Wardrobe of the Royal Household. The next set of parallel stone lines lead to the Lanthorn Tower, the end of the landward Wall.

A Roman Riverside Wall remained the stuff of myth until the mid-1970s when conclusive evidence was unearthed at Blackfriars. Discoveries made there correspond to the section of Roman Riverside Wall now part of the public display between the Lanthorn and the Wakefield Towers. The line of the Riverside Wall thereafter is punctuated by the Bell, the Byward and the Middle Towers, leaving the Tower precinct after the Tower Shop into Lower Thames Street.

Appendix II

Riverside Wall Walk

Keeping to the south side of Lower Thames Street, the stretch between Three Quays Wharf and the end of Custom House, represents the first leg of the Riverside Wall until about midway along the extended Custom House. Hereafter the line of the Wall dips to follow pretty much that of Lower Thames Street to about the junction with Byward Street. The Coal Exchange built in 1848 stood between St Dunstan's Hill and St Mary at Hill on the north side. In digging its foundations a Roman house with private baths was discovered, which was preserved and displayed within the basement of the building. Now 101 Lower Thames Street, work was in recent years carried out to improve public accessibility. At the time of writing, however, the building is empty and there are no event details available from the Museum of London. Further excavation work south of this site in the nineteenth century uncovered a solid Wall thought to be part of the Riverside Wall.

More masonry was found in 1911 between Monument Street and Pudding Lane close to a raft of oak and chestnut piles discovered in 1834 that may have been the foundations of the Riverside Wall. In the same year substantial masonry, presumed to be Roman, was discovered further west at the bottom of Fish Street Hill, and in 1912 more remains declared to be part of the Roman Riverside Wall were uncovered on the south side of the street. The previous year, while digging the foundations for 125 Lower Thames Street, large squared timbers supporting three layers of facing stones bonded with rows of yellow tiles were found.

During the building of St Magnus House in 1974, the Museum of London excavated a huge collection of Roman artefacts and an imposing timber quay, which was probably made redundant by the building of the Riverside Wall. The amount of material found here demonstrated London's prime purpose for most of the Roman occupation as a port.

The church of St Magnus the Martyr was founded around 1100 and stands on land originally reclaimed from the Thames foreshore by the Romans, when this port was established. A petrified Roman timber stump is displayed in the church porch together with a blackened fragment of Roman River Wall revetment. A blue plaque declares this site part of the route to the old London Bridge, several stones of which are also laid out in the churchyard. The first wooden bridge established by the Romans was replaced by Peter Colechurch's stone bridge in 1209, that lasted until the nineteenth century when a new bridge was started in 1823 and which was sold to American buyers in 1972.

After London Bridge, Lower Thames Street gives way to Upper Thames Street, where traces of the same type of quay construction (or Riverside Wall foundation) as that found at St Magnus House have been uncovered. More of what was considered to be remains of the Roman Riverside Wall were discovered in 1863, on the corner of Suffolk Lane opposite All Hallow's Lane to the left. This narrow passage leads to the Thameside Walk and Steelyard Passage, once the site of the walled community of the Hansa Merchants in London. Cannon Street Station has dominated this area since the 1850s, whereas in Roman times it was an imposing complex of buildings believed to have been the seat of central government.

After Cannon Street Station, on the north side of Upper Thames Street, Dowgate recalls one of the many ports, quays and water gates that came about after the fall of the Roman Riverside Wall. Slightly west was the outlet of the Walbrook River, Roman London's original harbour, with various quays along its line. In Roman times this minor waterway physically bisected the City from its source in Moorfields. Today it runs under the City discreetly disgorging its contents into the Thames from an outlet west of Cousin Lane.

At Southwark Bridge and the junction of Queen Street with Upper Thames Street, workmen digging a sewer opposite Vintners' Hall, came across 'the perfect remains of an old Roman wall, running parallel with the line of the river', which was similar in all respects to the other sections of Roman Wall uncovered thus far.

Cross here for the north side of Upper Thames Street and Queen Street. Take Skinner's Lane behind the Wren church of St James Garlickhythe to continue along the north side of Upper Thames Street. At the bottom of Lambeth Hill in 1841, a section of Wall 'of extraordinary strength' was uncovered that stretched from Blackfriars. The oak piles driven into the mud, the covering of chalk and stones, and the course of large hewn sandstones firmly cemented into place with quick lime, sand and pounded tile, comprised all the elements of the Riverside Wall. Subsequent excavations carried out in this area between the 1960s and 2003 have collectively identified a 'palatial administrative complex housing the primary functions of the late Roman state.' Possibly part of a massive programme of public works undertaken here included the Huggin Hill bathhouse and a massive podium for a temple.

St Mary Somerset Garden, with its surviving tower of the seventh-century Wren church, is where Upper Thames Street gives way to Castle Baynard Street, a long and dreary underpass that continues relentlessly to Puddle Dock where archaeological excavations in the 1970s finally established the existence of the Roman Riverside Wall. Follow the contour of The Mermaid Theatre around to the other side of Puddle Dock and the return to Blackfriars.

Bibliography

Barlow, Frank, *The Godwins: The Medieval World*. Longman, 2001

Bell, Walter G., Cottrill, M.A., Spon, Charles, *London Wall Through Eighteen Centuries*. (Council for Tower Hill Improvement), Balding and Mansell, 1937

Barton, Nicholas. *The Lost Rivers of London*. Phoenix House and Leicester University Press, 1962

Boatwright, Mary. T., *Hadrian and the Cities of the Roman Empire*. University Presses of California, Columbia and Princeton, 2002

Bradley, Timothy and Jonathan Butler, *From Temples to Thames Street – 2000 years of Riverside Development; Excavations at the Salvation Army International Headquarters, 99–101 Queen Victoria Street, City of London*. Pre-Construct Archaeology Monograph No. 7, 2008

Brown, Allen. R, *The Norman Conquest of England: Sources and Documents*. Boydell Press, 2002

Chapman, Hugh, Hall, Jenny and Marsh, Geoffrey. *The London Wall Walk*. Museum of London, 1985

Cook, Norman, *The Old Wall of the City of London*. Corporation of London, 1951

Davies, Hunter, *A Walk Along the Wall*. Weidenfield and Nicolson, 1974

Defoe, Daniel, *A Tour Through The While Island of Great Britain* (abridged), Yale University Press, 1991

———, *Journal of the Plague Year*. Penguin, 2003

———, *Colonel Jack*. Kessinger Publishing, 2004

Dyson, Tony (ed.), *The Roman Riverside Wall and Monumental Arch in London*. London and Middlesex Archaeological Society Special Paper No.3, 1980

Howe, Elizabeth and Lakin, David *Roman and Medieval Cripplegate, City of London: Archaeological Excavations 1992–8*. Museum of London Archaeology Service, 2004

Jones, David M., *Excavations at Billingsgate Buildings 'Triangle', Lower Thames Street 1974*. London, London & Middlesex Archaeological Society, 1986.

Lethaby, W.R. *Londinium. Architecture and the Crafts*. Duckworth & Co., 1923

Margary, I.D. *Roman Roads in Britain* (3rd edition). London, John Baker, 1973

Merrifield, Ralph, *London City of the Romans*. Batsford Ltd, 1983

Miller, Louise (John Schofield and Michael Rhodes), *The Roman quay at St Magnus House, London*. London, London & Middlesex Archaeological Society, 1986

Morris, John, *Londinium: London in the Roman Empire*. Weidenfield and Nicolson, 1982

Savage, Anne (Trans. and collated), *The Anglo-Saxon Chronicle*. Heinemann Ltd, 1983

Stenton, Sir Frank (Essay), Logan, Donald F. (Introduction), *Norman London by William Fitzstephen*. Italica Press, 1990

Stow, John. *A Survey of London written in the year 1598*. Alan Sutton, 1994

Webster, Norman W. *The Great North Road*. Adams and Dart, 1974

Williams, Dr Ann, and Morris, Professor G.H. *Domesday Book: A Complete Translation*. Penguin, 2003

Wood, Michael, *In Search of the Dark Ages*. BBC Books, 1987

Articles, Reports, Internet

Baker, T.F.T. 'A History of the County of Middlesex', Vol 10. 1995. Victoria County History Publication

Besant, Sir Walter, 'South London' Chatto & Windus 1899; London, 1901, new ed.

Bishop, M.C. 'The Camomile Street soldier reconsidered', Transactions of the London and Middlesex Archaeological Society, 1983

Butler, Jon. '100 years of the City Defences at Aldersgate'. *London Archaeologist*. Vol 9 No.9, Summer 2001

Corporation of London, Department of Planning: 'Newgate Conservation Area Character Summary.'

Corporation of London, Department of Planning, 'A Guide to the Riverside of the City of London and its future', 2001

———, 'Ludgate Hill Conservation Area Character Summary', 2001

———, 'Postman's Park Conservation Area Character Study', 2001

Corporation of London, 'The Official Guide to The Old Bailey', 1996

Department of Planning, Central Criminal Court 'The Church of St Sepulchre, 15 Old Bailey, Newgate Street, Snow Hill Giltspur Street', Newgate, 1999

Gordon, Lewis Dunbar Brodie, 'A short description of the plans of Captain I. Vetch, for the sewerage of the Metropolis', 1851

Harben, Henry A. 'Dictionary of London 1918'. Centre for Metropolitan History Publication

Leigh, Samuel, 'A new picture of London, or, A view of the political, religious, medical, literary, municipal, commercial, and moral state of the British metropolis: presenting a luminous guide to the stranger, on all subjects connected with general information, business, or amusement : to which are subjoined a description of the environs, and a plan for viewing London in eight days' 1834. London: Leigh and Son, Baldwin and Cradock

Noorthouck, John, 'A New History of London, 1773'. Centre for Metropolitan History

Page, William, 'A History of the County of London: 1909' County History Publication

Price, J.E. 'On a Bastion of London Wall, or, Excavations in Camomile Street, Bishopsgate, London', 1880

Rees, Christine. 'All Hallow London Wall: A Short History', Christian Aid London & South East Team, 2000

Strype, John, 'A Survey of the Cities of London Westminster, 1720'. Humanities Research Institute, The University of Sheffield

Thornbury, Walter, 'Old and New London, 1878' Centre for Metropolitan History

Watson, Bruce, MOLAS, 'King Edward Buildings, former Royal Mail Sorting Office, Giltspur & Newgate Street, EC1', TQ 3190 8144, June 1998-January 1999.

Webster, Norman W. *The Great North Road*. Adams and Dart, 1974

Wilson, John Marius, 'Imperial Gazetteer of England and Wales', 1870–72

List of Illustrations

It is with grateful thanks that permission has been granted for the following photographs and illustrations to appear in this publication. Every effort has been made to contact the known and perceived copyright holders, their assigns or heirs. Where it can be shown that a copyholder's right has been infringed then every effort will be made by the author to make up for any breach of that right. Where no accreditation is attached, the illustrations and images more imperfect in execution are entirely the responsibility of the author.

1 Photograph of London Wall, Trinity Place, 1882. P. Norman, from *London Wall Through Eighteen Centuries,* 1937
2 Map of City of London and London Wall
3 Diagram showing composition of London Wall from *Roman London*, reproduced in *London Wall Through Eighteen Centuries,* 1937
4 Diagram of example bastion at Le Mans and Senlis reproduced from *Londinium, Architecture and the Crafts,* 1923
5 Photograph of Temple Bar, 2008
6 Map of Blackfriars to Ludgate Hill
7 Photograph of Fleet Valley Project, Pilgrim Street looking west, reproduced by kind permission of Bill McCann
8 Photograph of Fleet Valley Project, South face, reproduced by kind permission of Bill McCann
9 Photograph of Fleet Valley Project, Pilgrim Street looking south, reproduced by kind permission of Bill McCann
10 Photograph of rubble Wall, St Anne's Church, Blackfriars, 2008
11 Map of Ludgate to Newgate, 2008
12 Illustration of Medieval Tower discovered south of Ludgate Hill, 1792, from J.T. Smith's *Antient Topography* reproduced in *London Wall Through Eighteen Centuries,* 1937
13 Illustration of Ludgate burning in the Great Fire of 1666 from Wilkinson's *Londina Illustrata* reproduced in *London Wall Through Eighteen Centuries,* 1937
14 Photograph of Sessions House Wall, Amen Court, 2008

15 Photograph of Roman Wall exposed on the site of Newgate Prison in 1903 from *London Wall Through Eighteen Centuries,* 1937

16 Photograph of Roman Wall in the basement of Central Criminal Court, Old Bailey, 1992, compliments of the Corporation of London

17 Map of Newgate to Aldersgate, 2008

18 Photograph of City Wall remains at Merrill Lynch HQ. Image copyright Graham Gaunt, 2008

19 Photograph of bastion remains at Merrill Lynch HQ. Image copyright Graham Gaunt, 2008

20 Map from Aldersgate to Moorgate, 2008

21 Photograph of south-west corner of the Roman Fort and City Wall, Noble Street, 2008

22 Photograph of culvert, south west corner of the Roman fort and City Wall, Noble Street, 2008. p.100

23 Photograph of Roman fort west wall and Plasterers' Hall, Noble Street, 2008

24 Photograph of Roman fort west wall by London Wall, 2008

25 Photograph of Roman fort West Gate, London Wall, 2008. Reproduced with the kind permission of the Corporation of London

26 Photograph of West Wall Monkwell Street bastion, south side, 2008

27 Photograph of West Wall Monkwell Street bastion, north side, 2008

28 Photograph of West Wall Barber Surgeon's Hall bastion, 2008

29 Photograph of West Wall Barber Surgeon's Hall bastion interior, 2008

30 Nineteenth-century illustration of Cripplegate Bastion, St Giles' churchyard from J.W. Archer's *Vestiges of Old London* reproduced in *London Wall Through Eighteen Centuries,* 1937

31 Twenty-first century photograph of Cripplegate Bastion, St Giles' Churchyard. Andy Wadden, 2008

32 Photograph of Cripplegate bastion interior. Andy Wadden, 2008

33 Photograph of Roman fort north wall bastion foundation. Andy Wadden, 2008

34 Photograph of Roman fort north wall remains. Andy Wadden, 2008

35 Nineteenth-century illustration of the last remains of Cripplegate Postern from *Vestiges of Old London* reproduced in *London Wall Through Eighteen Centuries,* 1937

36 Photograph of London Wall in St Alphage churchyard, 2008

37 Photograph of Salters' Garden. Andy Wadden, 2008

38 Photograph of St Alphage tower, London Wall, 2008

39 Map from Moorgate to Bishopsgate, 2008

40 Photograph of London Wall, All Hallows-on-the-Wall, 2008

41 Map from Bishopsgate to Aldgate, 2008

42 Plan of Camomile Street bastion recorded in 1876. Published by J.E. Price, 1880

43 Map of Aldgate to Tower Hill, 2008

44 Photograph of London Wall remains 3, Jewry Street (east), 2008

45 Photograph of London Wall remains 3, Jewry Street (west), 2008

46 Photograph of Roman Wall in the cellar of Roman Wall House, No 1 Crutched Friars in 1936 from *The Old Wall of the City of London*

47 Photograph of Roman Wall in the Departure Bar, Roman Wall House, No 1 Crutched Friars. Reproduced by kind permission of the Departure Bar, 2008

Index

Visit our website and discover thousands of other History Press books.

www.thehistorypress.co.uk